THE BEAST AND I

PAUL CROWTHER

Edited by Jonathan Downes
Cover and internal design by Mark North for CFZ Communications
Using Microsoft Word 2000, Microsoft Publisher 2000, Adobe Photoshop CS.

Photographs © 2005 Paul Crowther/Chris Moiser except where noted

First published in Great Britain by CFZ Press

CFZ Press is a division of:

CFZ Communications
15 Holne Court,
Exwick,
Exeter.
EX4 2NA

© CFZ 2005

All rights reserved. Without limiting the rights under copyright reserved above, no part of this publication may be reproduced, stored in or introduced into a retrieval system, or transmitted, in any form of by any means (electronic, mechanical, photocopying, recording or otherwise), without the prior written permission of both the copyright owners and the publishers of this book.

ISBN: 0-9512872-4-9

ACKNOWLEDGEMENTS

I would like to take this opportunity to thank all those involved in getting this into your hands, especially Iwona Crowther - wonder-wife, super tec, and saint; the OLD FOLKS - the OLD MAN for crisp story and the OLD DOLL for being as mad as a spoon, Chris Moiser, (me best mate), Mr Kuczynski; for the superb cartoons, the bods at the CFZ, and finally Mike Thomas.

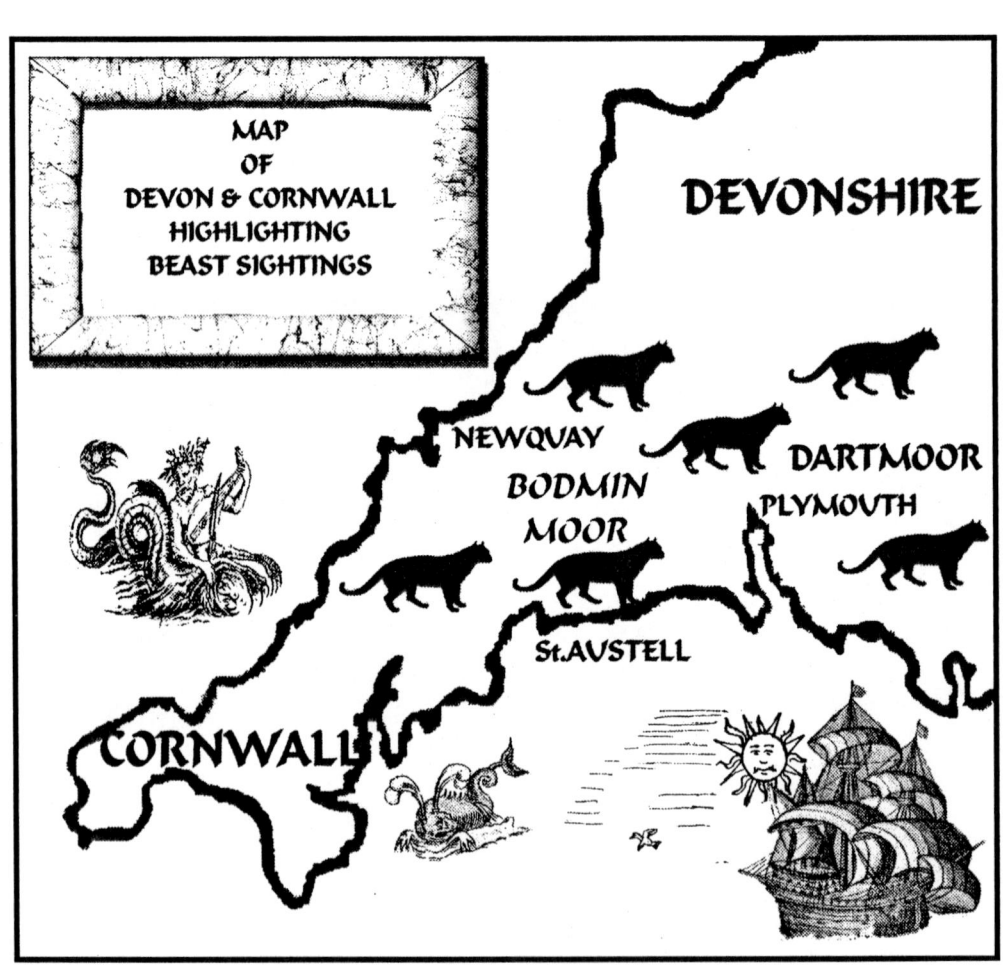

CONTENTS

FOREWORD BY MIKE THOMAS..	7
INTRODUCTION...	9
FROM QUIET BEGINNINGS TO ZOO PHOTOGRAPHER...............	11
NOW I AM - PAUL CROWTHER "BEAST OF BODMIN" IMAGE DEBUNKER!..	19
COULD THIS BE A RAT I SMELL..	27
SKY'S THE LIMIT...	29
AN INSIDER'S VIEW OF THE "BEAST CONFERENCE"...............	37
SOMEONE GET THAT BLOODY PHONE!...................................	45
FEMALE VICARS AND FARMERS (WELL IT MAKES A CHANGE FROM VICARS AND TARTS)	47
THE ZOOKEEPER'S REVENGE AND STRANGE BOXES?............	53
"LARA" THE LYNX OF LONDON TOWN......................................	59
TWO YOKELS GO TO WONDERLAND AND ONE HAS AN ULTERIOR MOTIVE FOR GOING (2002)...	65
TO WONDERLAND AND BACK AGAIN: THE CONTINUING STORY OF TWO YOKELS (2003)	75
ARE WE SAD OR WOT..	81
HAS THE CAT COME BACK?...	83
CAN YOU LOOK AT OUR VIDEO?...	89
LITTLE PRICKS AND A SHAG OR - AUGUST COMES EARLY IN 2002 FOR THE CORNISH GUARDIAN..	91
IS THIS THE LAST OF MIKE THOMAS?......................................	95
THE USUAL SUSPECTS...	99
10000000010000001 ANALYSE THAT!...................................	103
CATASTROPHE...	107
IT IS NOT JUST THE CORNISH, YOU KNOW! EVERYONE WANTS ONE!...	111
THE LAND OF WIZARDS, WITCHES AND DRAGONS TRIES TO ADD BIG CATS TO ITS LIST OF TOURIST ATTRACTIONS............	117

Foreword

by
Mike Thomas

(Former Owner of Newquay Zoo, Current Owner of Canonteign Falls & Big Cat and "Beast" Expert)

The idea of Big Cats roaming around Britain captivates people's imagination in the same way as the mystery of the Loch Ness Monster and Ghosts – all of which I am a firm believer in. As a recognised "expert" in Big Cats, especially the behaviour of those in the wild, I have had to suffer my fair share of critics who - whilst supporting my beliefs, spend time dissecting my evidence and theories. Paul Crowther - a fellow believer - has cast a critical eye and raised questions of doubt at what I have reported on many occasions, none more so than when I first met him eight years ago when I launched filmed evidence of "big cats" on the loose in Cornwall. He doubted what he saw, stating that the cat seemed to be domestic and small. As I told him: Big cats start life as small cats. He was not convinced of my wisdom on this occasion.

However all of us who dare to offer opinions, evidence and theories about sightings and the existence of these animals leave ourselves wide open to criticism and sometimes "good hearted" ridicule. Wherever there is an element of doubt there are doubters. My now good friend Paul, has investigated sightings with me many times. Whilst we are both believers in the existence of these cats, we are able to accept and deliver "light hearted" banter since we have shared many fascinating and hilarious experiences in our search for the "Beast".

This book does much to highlight our interest in the continuing search for the "Beast" and I am delighted to remain involved in such an important project.

Mike Thomas

INTRODUCTION

There comes a time in every man's life, when he is forced to reflect on his position and status relative to life, the universe and everything. My epiphany came in the usual manner for a married man; via my wife!

Iwona, because that's my wife's name, is a woman of rare insight when it comes to assessing a person's character. Iwona turned to me while we were driving home one evening after a celebrity photo shoot and exclaimed, "You are turning into a very sad person!" Or words to that effect.

Even though I am her husband, I had to agree that her assessment was accurate. We had gone to the BBC Studios in Plymouth with a group of students to photograph the local TV presenters for 'Children in Need'. Despite being suitably impressed with meeting these celebrities, the most exciting part of the "shoot" for me was finding Darky the cat from next door to the BBC in the car park.

Darky, I must explain, plays an important part in my alter egos' life, that of Paul Crowther, "Beast of Bodmin" image debunker. The BBC had used Darky as the bullets to shoot down a local zookeeper's video footage of the "Beast of Bodmin" back in July 1998. The BBC had put a split screen on the television, and then asked Mike Thomas to distinguish between the zoos' video, and the BBCs footage of Darky the cat, on their 6.30pm news bulletin

So how had I gone from a happy-go-lucky laboratory technician, to a sad obsessive who gets excited about meeting a moggy in the BBC's car park, in the space of twelve years?

FROM QUIET BEGINNINGS TO ZOO PHOTOGRAPHER

I started working at a large College of Further Education in the spring of 1988 as a laboratory technician and part-time photographic lecturer.

This was, what I can in hindsight describe, as my happy time. Life was simple - well, simple from the photographic standpoint. All I had to do was teach, put the students portfolios in for examination, and ensure that the students turned up for their written examinations and - Hey Presto - they all passed.

1993 could be accurately described as my "*Annus Cockupus*". If I had been as clever as I would like to think I am, I should have seen it was going to be a train at the end of the tunnel, not a light! Things started in a low key manner, as befits events that make you turn left, when you should have turned right, at one of life's little cross-roads.

All I had to do was photograph students and volunteers building a conservation area. You see, the Biology section had commandeered an area of wasteland on the College's campus, and set about converting it into an award winning conser-

vation area. Photographing the transformation was enjoyable, and the Biology lecturers were happily using my photographs as evidence to successfully apply for grants and awards.

While this was going on, the Zoology lecturer kept turning up with his students, fertling about looking for wildlife, (the wildlife, it transpired, was mainly bugs and biddies, but the lecturer seemed happy enough with his discoveries).

Then it happened – it was a classic manoeuvre, better even than the Greeks and their wooden horse. The Zoologist (one Chris Moiser), engaged me in conversation just as I was in the middle of washing-up after a particularly large experiment. By the time the last beaker had been washed, I had agreed to accompany Chris and his students on a Zoology field trip to Shaldon Wildlife Park to take photographs of the students and their activities.

Shaldon is a small zoo which deals mainly with small mammals like marmosets. These are ideal for students to study animal behaviour, and from my point of view they were of sufficient interest for me to spend the day photographing them. Two days later I was in my preparation room examining the fruits of my labours at Shaldon, when Chris came into the room to look at the pictures.

If you are going to get the attention of a person for any reason at all, the first line of attack is - flattery. Tell a woman that she looks good, has lost weight etc, and they are yours. When Chris told me that my photographs of the marmosets were very good, despite my turning up my nose at his comments, he knew he had a friend for life.

Payback time came quicker than I expected. In fact it took less than two hours. Again his attack was timed to perfection; just after lunch! Apparently Chris had these friends called John and Joy Palmer who owned a zoo called Porfell Animal Land. Porfell had been going for a few years and they had some interesting exhibits called Baz and Amy (a pair of caracals) and Joy and John needed some photographs for postcards and advertising, and what was more, I could go in the cages with the animals if I was brave enough!

The nerve of the man, not content with the flattery approach, he threw in a challenge to my masculinity as well. Caracals! Pahh I'd have gone into the lion's den without the assistance of Daniel!

So the following weekend, I found myself being presented to John and Joy as the photographic expert from the college. The only odd thing about this first meeting was that Chris did not inform me that Joy had actually married Father Christmas, and we had discovered him doing his summer job. I mean, the evidence was there for all to see - flowing white locks and the largest white beard I

had ever seen. Well the largest white beard since the last time I saw "John" in Lewis's in Liverpool sometime around Christmas 1964. Even John's attempt to conceal his true identity was not that good – he was carrying a spade, wearing a bush hat, baggy shorts, and a tee shirt.

"You've been mucking out the reindeer, haven't you?" I offered. You could have knocked me over with a feather when he answered in the affirmative. After a bit of a chat, John then gave me a list of combinations for the enclosures locks that it was safe for me to photograph in.

So Chris, Iwona and I set off for the first enclosure; that of the chipmunks. Iwona opened the lock, and ushered me in. "How did you remember the combination?" I queried. "Photographic memory" came the response.

By now, you may have gathered, I am a simple soul, easily confused by the every day vagaries of life, but here I was, about to go into an enclosure containing twenty-seven chipmunks, and in the past five minutes, I had not only seen through the disguise of Father Christmas, but discovered that my wife had a photographic memory!

I pretended to fumble around in my camera bag looking for an appropriate roll of film. I offered up a silent prayer of thanks to Mr. Nikon for the `hunting mode auto focus` on my camera. At the same time I was watching the demented chipmunks run around their cage. This eccentric behaviour was obviously because the chipmunks thought it was feeding time. Why else would someone open the outer door?

As I loaded the camera, Chris and Iwona started coming out with barbed comments and questioning my masculinity. This was it! No turning back now; in I went.

For my first close encounter I felt it went rather well - well, to a point. Iwona started it, but it didn't take Chris long to join in. "It's behind you, don't put your foot down, it's after your nuts, do you want some cooling oil for your auto focus it's beginning to smoke!" Now I can take a joke as well as the next man, but the sight of two thirty-year olds rolling round the floor yelling something like;"get him out of there before I wet myself", does not do a great deal for one's ego. However, looking on the bright side, I was drawing rather a large crowd and despite having to remove a chipmunk that had been trying to build a nest in my hair, I felt that I had retained my composure and dignity, as I exited the enclosure.

Iwona locked up the enclosure and Chris, who had taken it upon himself to become the crowd's official guide, was informing the multitude that I was going to

photograph the coatis next! And they are bigger than chipmunks.

I was ushered into the coati cage by my eye-shadow-smudged wife. A roar went up as I came into the view of an expectant crowd. Chris was whipping the crowd to a frenzy, as he gave them the complete history of the coati. Like all good performers, I naturally acknowledged my growing audience, then I turned to see just what it was that I was going to attempt to photograph.

I was greeted by a nicely framed group of mum coati, dad and baby. A more intelligent man than me would have realised that mum was not too pleased to see a stranger in the enclosure, and that she was beginning to make ominous noises. Now a coati is not that threatening a sight. They can in a certain light, look quite cute with their longish noses. However, when you are looking at these animals through a 70 – 210mm lens, they do tend to appear slightly larger and more vicious than they are in real life, and I was now looking at a very aggravated family. I had taken a few frames when it happened – there was a very loud bang from somewhere directly above my head. That was it -I was off.

Visibly shaken, I was out of the cage faster than the proverbial rat up a drainpipe. As I stood there shaking, so were the crowd, only they were all shaking with laughter. It appears that a very large male peacock had landed on the roof of the enclosure at exactly the instant I had filled the viewfinder with a full frontal of mummy coatis teeth.

I needed time to recover, but no - Chris was off, directing the crowd to the genet enclosure. Fortunately for me, the unsuspecting duo were curled up in a ball together fast asleep. Chris hushed the crowd so as not to wake the slumbering genets, and give them warning that Dr. Disaster was about to enter their peaceful world.

Great, the dynamic duo had picked the most inaccessible area of the enclosure to have their siesta. However, with some dexterity on my part, I got the shot I wanted, and even better the genets were still asleep. Success!

Well, in a word – No. Flushed with the success of taking the pictures without disturbing the genets, I stood up and promptly started seeing stars! I had smacked my head on a very large branch that was part of the structure that supported the platform on which the genets were sleeping. As I staggered around, the genets bolted for the safety of their indoor enclosure, while I, in an effort not to step on them in my near concussed state, managed to pull down the rest of the poor animal's outdoor activity centre.

The crowd was going wild as Iwona and Chris led me away to the coffee shop to recover, and I distinctly remember hearing a little child saying to his father:

"This is better than the circus you took us to last year".

As I sat there recovering, and apologising profusely to John about demolishing the genet's enclosure, Iwona and Chris went off to see Baz and Amy. When they returned, Iwona kept dangling her fingers in front of her mouth saying, "They've got very big pointy teeth, and they're bigger than I thought," and sucking air in through her teeth and shaking her head at the same time.

I must have looked rough, because the group started to carry out some medical tests on me. While I thought that I was being smart by saying there were more fingers being shown than there actually were, the group then took a unanimous decision that I did not look well enough to risk going into the enclosure with the two caracals, and everyone would be happier if we came back the following weekend to finish the job.

The following weekend was an absolute belter. The sun was cracking the paving stones, and there wasn't a cloud in the sky. Iwona and I arrived at Porfell early, so that if there were to be any disasters like the previous week, they would at least be carried out in private. Joy and John pounced on my photographs from my first visit, and declared themselves suitably impressed with them.

So to the caracal enclosure. John came into the cage with me. Baz was sitting perched high up on a platform in a tree surveying his kingdom when we entered, and Amy was eating the remains of a chicken at ground level. My first impression of these wonderful lynx-like cats was that they were Welsh! I mean this as a compliment. Caracals are relatively short, stocky, and very powerful - a bit like a Welsh prop forward if you get my meaning. In my opinion, caracals are not as graceful or feline in their movements as other exotic cats that I have photographed, but they definitely look as if they could do a lot of damage if they ever got hold of you.

Intent on capturing these feline bulldozers on film, I wedged myself into a corner and started snapping away. Allegedly, Amy strolled over and sniffed the air a few inches from me, but I was too engrossed in taking the pictures to notice. Anyway, John was with me just in case anything serious were about to happen. If you can't trust Father Christmas to look out for you, who can you trust?

As we headed for a coffee, John commented on my coolness while I was being checked out by Amy. I confessed that I hadn't even noticed her. John went on to tell me about events earlier in the week. Apparently, two students from the local Art College, turned up to photograph the cats, and while they were photographing Amy had done the same crotch smelling exercise to one of the students as she had done to me. Unfortunately, the student's reaction was rather different to mine – Allegedly there was this unfortunate smell, and the photo shoot had to be

abandoned!

One of the joys of being in education, is that occasionally you are involved in life changing events for students. Rob was one of Chris's students, who with the assistance of a Nuffield bursary, Chris had managed to place on secondment with Danny and Lyn at Exmoor Zoological Gardens in North Devon. Rob had spent several weeks studying the behaviour of Ring Tailed Lemurs, and as a means of re-payment, Nuffield were going to use photographs of Rob as an example of the uses their bursary could be put to.

It appears that the foundation had sent a photographer to the Gardens to photograph Rob and the lemurs. Unfortunately his films were severely damaged - as a direct result of them being excessively exposed to lemur widdle - and so the foundation needed the photographs taken again.

I was pleased for the opportunity to work for such a prestigious organisation, Chris and I joked about the original photographers misfortune all the way to Barnstaple. Lyn, Danny, Rob and `Buster` (the Gardens free-roaming penguin), greeted us at the entrance. Owing to the distances involved in travelling to and from Barnstaple, I decided it would be better if the shoot took place sooner rather than later, as ominous rain clouds were gathering overhead. Remembering what had happened to the previous photographer, I loaded my camera up outside the cage, and left the camera bag safely outside the cage. No lemur or lemurs for that matter were going to flood my camera bag out with their widdle. No Sir!

The lemurs were stunning to photograph, and they had obviously taken a liking to Rob. I took picture after picture; as they ran to him, as he fed them by hand with their favourite food. Suddenly there was this yell from Chris of "Gerr out of it!" I spun around to see what was the cause of the commotion. I had turned just in time to see a very disgruntled Buster dismount my camera bag! It appears the sight of my camera bag just lying there was too much for this short-sighted, sexually frustrated penguin.

To make matters worse for the penguin - not only did he fail to mate with the object of his desire, but everyone was laughing at him as he slowly waddled away from the scene of his failed conquest.

Based on these experiences, people now think that as well as being a photographic teacher, I have become a zoo photographer, and based on people believing that I am a zoo photographer, a new chapter in my life was about to unfold.

NOW I AM – PAUL CROWTHER "BEAST OF BODMIN" IMAGE DEBUNKER!

Strange things started happening at the `China Fleet Golf and Country Club` in the summer of 1994. Golfers started appearing in the local newspapers, and on local television; because of their golfing prowess? No. Apparently they were seeing a large black, leopard-type cat, that casually strolled across the fairways and greens at the far end of the course!

Now, unbeknown to me, Chris had written this article in the local paper on the subject of exotic cats, and as a result of his seeming-expert knowledge, the club manager invited Chris to come and give his expert opinion on the sightings that had been taking place on the course. Once again, the Machiavellian side of Chris revealed itself; instead of saying he needed a lift to go to the China Fleet Club, he told me to go home and get my camera, because we were going on a leopard hunt!

Suitably equipped with a camera, Chris, David O'Sullivan (Club manager) and

myself headed for the unraked bunkers surrounding the seventh green. As a golfer, my first impression was that someone at the club did not know golf etiquette, as the bunker was a mess.

To say that Chris lost all self-control might be over-stating the excitement he displayed as he looked at the scene that greeted us. "Look, look just look at these" he almost screeched as he gesticulated wildly at the mess. "Photograph that!" he said, pointing. At this stage in the proceedings, Chris must have realised that I was not exactly up to speed with the amazing sight I was beholding – "These are the tracks of a very large cat – a leopard or a puma". Now if my mate Chris says that the tracks are of a puma, who am I a mere Laboratory technician, part-time photographic lecturer, and sometime zoo photographer to question him?

When I finished photographing the evidence! Chris and David went into a huddle. "Right, lets go see if we can find ourselves a big cat! Keep close Paul". The other two decided that it would be a good idea to check out the wooded copse that ran along side the seventh fairway. David, having been in the forces, organised us so that he led the way; Chris was in the middle, looking up in case the "Beast" came at us from out of the trees, and I was to walk backwards in case the "Beast" decided to attack us from the rear.

What we looked like I hate to think, and anyone watching us could have been excused for bursting into uncontrollable laughter. Every time David stopped, Chris bumped into him because he was scanning the overhanging branches, and I just flattened the pair of them as I was walking backwards.

The further we went into the copse the more nervous the tension became and then it happened – there was a rapid movement in the long grass and whatever it was appeared to be coming straight for us! We froze, then a rabbit shot straight between Chris and myself. That was it. I was off—more out of necessity than anything else.

In the bar afterwards I congratulated David on the excellent facilities in the Gentlemen's toilet, and promised him that I would praise them at every opportunity I got. Over a cup of steaming hot chocolate, Chris explained that there had been numerous reported sightings of a large exotic cat in the past. In Cornwall it was referred to as the "Beast of Bodmin", and Chris was convinced that there was definitely an increase in the number of sightings.

Chris was a wealth of information when it came to the "Beast". He explained the history behind the various sightings. Allegedly, two policemen who were having a surreptitious Chinese takeaway at the Calstock roundabout, had actually seen the "Beast" - sitting in the middle of the roundabout watching the traf-

UNIVERSITY LECTURER POURS SCORN ON WILDCAT THEORY

Beast 'is just two pet cats'

MOGGIE OR WILD CAT? This picture of the 'Beast' was supplied courtesy of the Cornish Guardian. **INSET** Our blown up picture shows what Beast hunter Chris Moiser says could be two domestic cats

BY WILLIAM TELFORD

A PLYMOUTH biology lecturer claims a recently published picture of the so-called Beast of Bodmin Moor is a photo of two house cats.

Plymouth College of Further Education lecturer Chris Moiser – himself a beast-hunter – said the cat is a marmalade moggy, and behind it is a curled up tabby.

He said both he and CFE colleague Paul Crowther, a photography lecturer, have serious doubts about the photo, supposedly taken last Christmas near St Austell.

But the newspaper editor who first published the snap, Cornish Guardian supremo Alan Cooper, said the picture is genuine and has vowed to publish another one in the paper this Thursday.

Unconvinced Chris said: "They are domestic cats. Although the tail is suspiciously wide for a domestic cat, the face is that of a domestic cat. And it's abdomen is distorted from having multiple kittens."

Chris, from Stoke, said he doesn't think the cat is either a strange new breed of feline, or a cross-breed.

Unlikely

He explained: "The chance of finding a new species is highly unlikely. The last new species found was the irimote cat found on a remote island off Japan in 1967.

"In this country there is a hybrid, which is a cross between a Scottish wild cat and a domestic cat, but they are all black, so it's not one of these."

Chris, who investigated sightings of a cat-like creature prowling near Saltash a few years ago, says he thinks big cats are loose in the West Country – but this picture is not one.

He said: "I believe there are exotic cats living wild, possibly puma. A lot of people have reported lynx too, but a leopard is harder to believe."

But Alan Cooper maintains the picture is genuine, and says the man who took it, who he is not naming, will take him to the spot where the photo was shot.

He said Mr Moiser's views were 'full of opinion and light on fact'.

He added: "I have a negative of the animal moving away and will publish that. I wouldn't have published the first one if I wasn't positive it's genuine. These people are trying to debunk it, but I've got proof."

...and so it begins

Second picture of mystery creature published after college lecturers question first photograph

Bid to silence puma doubts

A SECOND picture of the puma-like animal seen recently in Cornwall has been released to silence doubters who claim the first shot was a fake.

The new picture published – like the original – by the Cornish Guardian shows the animal moving away to its left.

It is the next frame in the roll of film taken near St Austell by a photographer who has asked for his identity and the location to be kept secret.

The pictures of the puma-like creature were taken using a camera through a pair of binoculars. This is why the new picture has a rounded appearance.

The publication of this new evidence follows efforts by two Plymouth lecturers to cast doubts on the authenticity of the original.

Chris Moiser, a biology lecturer at Plymouth College of Further Education, and colleague Paul Crowther, a photography lecturer, say the picture of the golden-coloured animal is "not a specimen in its entirety".

They have a drawn up a list of objections to the first photo, which they describe as "suspicious for a number of reasons" – although they do not doubt it was published in good faith.

In a long letter to the editor of the Cornish Guardian, Alan Cooper, the pair say the two animals in the first photo are actually domestic cats. They say the perspective and shadows cast in the picture are wrong, and question why no area is in focus.

The neck and tail of the cat appear to the authors to be "unnaturally" stretched.

"The face is not that of a puma but is similar to that of a large marmalade domestic cat or a medium-sized exotic cat such as a caracal," the pair write.

But Mr Cooper has hit back, saying: "One can argue about what sort of animals they are but they are certainly not common moggies. The letter from Messrs Moiser and Crowther is staggering in its pomposity and arrogance. It is heavy on opinion but very light on fact.

"I cannot treat seriously two academics who have reached conclusions about a picture when they have not seen the negatives. What sort of research is that?

"Why didn't they ask to see them as other experts have?

"I think this is a huge case of sour grapes."

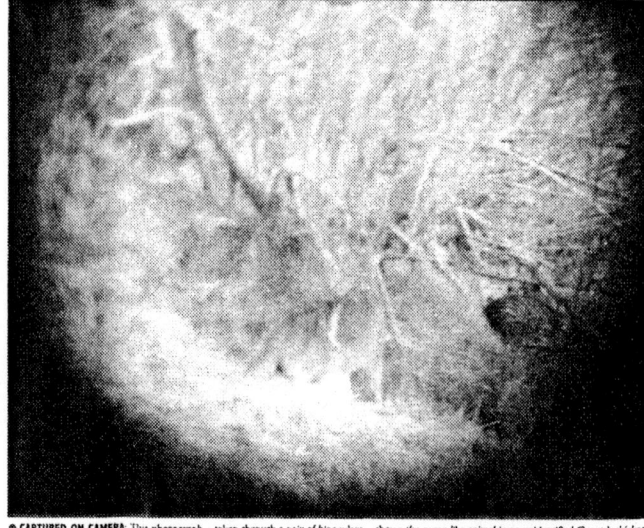

● **CAPTURED ON CAMERA:** This photograph – taken through a pair of binoculars – shows the puma-like animal in an unidentified Cornish thicket

THE SUN, Friday, January 7, 1994 15

THE BEAST'S BACK

Sun reader finds puma

A GIANT cat takes a drink from floodwater — dramatic proof that the Beast of Bodmin is back.

Sun reader Keith Farmer stumbled across the creature near his home.

Electrician Keith, 37, took

EXCLUSIVE by NEIL SYSON

two snaps — then ran out of film on his simple point-and-shoot 35mm camera.

He was "shocked and excited" by the encounter in the hamlet of Fenton Pits, near Lanlivet, Cornwall.

It was just 15 miles from Palmersbridge where a Sun photographer snapped the puma-like beast last October.

Keith said: "I saw this thing 400 yards away. It was at least 3ft long, with a tail as long again, and about knee high."

The Beast has been blamed for a series of savage cattle killings on the moorland.

The so-called "Beast of Lanlivet"

fic. Unfortunately, they could not officially report the sighting, as they should not have been there in the first place, and they definitely should not have been eating the Chinese takeaway.

Some way through his potted history of "Beast" sightings, he casually mentioned the time that a national newspaper had offered a £1,000 reward for the carcass of the "Beast of Exmoor". This resulted in every gun owner and his granny turning up to look for the "Beast". Needless to say, the police soon put a stop to that and the following day the paper modified their reward to being for a photograph of the "Beast" instead of the carcass.

I went home and slept on the news that there was potentially £1,000 for a fake photograph of the "Beast of Bodmin Moor."

As a teacher, I tell my students that every picture they take is a factual record of an event, person, place or thing at a given time in history. But, the camera does lie, or rather the photographer/photographic printer can make the camera lie. In the latter part of the 19th and early years of the 20th century these were works of art, and I really mean works of art, produced by highly skilled crafts people. I used examples like Rejlanders' "two ways of life" which involved his manipulating over thirty individual images into one panoramic image of piety and debauchery. Then there was the blatant re-working of history by Stalin. The work of the technicians working on the images exhibited during Stalin's' reign makes David Blaine look like a second rate conjurer, seldom have so many people disappeared and locations changed. The more I thought about it, the more convinced I was that a minimum of a "grand" was a big incentive to fake an image of the "Beast of Bodmin". As the subject of the "Beast" was new to me, it led me to wonder how many people knew of the "Beast's" existence, and more importantly how many knew about the reward?

I brought the subject up with my next class by posing the question: What do you know of the `Beast of Bodmin`? I know that you can get a lot of money from an image of it, came the reply. On further discussion it appeared that this student's daughter and her boyfriend had faked one of the more famous images of a Cornish big-cat - the "Lanlivet Beast" image - using a cardboard cut-out, and got paid for it!

It appears that this girl and her then boyfriend took photographs of their cut-out `"Beast"` in black and white. This is very important, because it meant that they had total control over the image production from the negative development through to the final image that they were going to present to the world. The intrepid duo, however, had several problems to overcome.

The first - and perhaps the most important - worry, was the potential of obtain-

ing monies under false pretences. To counter this, his or her cut-out had a ridiculously long tail, and looked so deformed that anyone looking at the picture should have questioned just what it was a picture of.

Their second problem was that of scale. To overcome this, they photographed the cut-out in the middle of a field beside a pond with no reference points in the image. This meant there was nothing in the image to compare the "Beast" with; therefore there was nothing to get a comparison of size with, so the "Beast" could have been any size the imagination wanted it to be!

The final problem they had to overcome was that of reality: unfortunately, their image looked a little too much like a cut-out. To counter this they came up with an ingenious solution: Just as the enlarger was about to finish exposing the image, they tapped the side of the machine. The result is an image that looks as if it has camera shake; shake appropriately induced by the excitement of seeing the "Beast of Bodmin!"

I must confess I was relatively shocked at the candidness of this revelation, although I did have a sneaking admiration for the perpetrators of this cunning plan. I was especially impressed in the way they had attempted to overcome the photographic technicalities involved in producing a deliberately blurred final print.

So now, thanks to Chris, I had discovered that there was a whole cottage industry of photographers in Devon and Cornwall all trying to - well, without putting too fine a point on it - con the British press out of a considerable sum of money.

For some mysterious reason I got very pious and was filled with an urge to protect the great British public from these charlatans! My pious attitude could have had something to do with the burgeoning popularity of the photographer's new toys – the digital camera and digital manipulation. At this time, some people were beginning to express some concern about the use of computer images in national newspapers.

It would appear that even the pyramids had changed their location in some photographs printed in newspapers. The arguments still carry on today, although the arguments now tend to be about the preservation of history.

The first opportunity for me to express my suspicions over the authenticity of a "Beast" image came in December 1997. The Cornish Guardian had acquired what it described as the definitive image of "the Beast". Chris and I looked at the image and decided to go on the attack. I must confess I felt that the image had been doctored with the assistance of a computer, while Chris thought it was the most peculiar "Beast" he had ever seen. So, we challenged the editor over

the validity of the image.

We pointed out in a long letter to the paper just what we thought of the image, from the photographic content and the physiological perspective of `the "Beast"`. To say the editor did not like that is putting it mildly. The following week Chris and I were absolutely panned; we were dubbed `Mr Pompous` and `Mr Arrogant`; the editor also gave a long list of experts who backed up his standpoint that he had published an image of "The Beast of Bodmin". Now, both parties were treading on dubious ground. We demanded the right to see the negatives, and if we were proved right, then the editors' experts were going to look extremely silly. Unfortunately, some of these experts were highly respected in their field of knowledge, and Chris and I were just mere teachers!

After much discussion between the two of us, we felt we were in a no-win situation, but that we had to press our arguments. A meeting was arranged between the editor, his staff and ourselves. We turned up with all the portable equipment I could muster, which would allow both parties to be satisfied that a full investigation had taken place.

The first interesting fact to come out of the meeting was that there was more than just the one image. The editor had not published the other images because he felt that they would have given the location of the "Beast site" away! The second surprise was that the images had been taken through a pair of binoculars placed in front of the camera lens; a point, I think, that showed incredible ingenuity on the part of the photographer.

The images were transferred onto a large television, and the investigation began. Despite the enormity of the televised image I could not find any evidence of digital manipulation; one nil to the paper! However the unpublished images swung the argument totally in Chris's and my favour. The cat had been photographed in front of a brick wall, and by simple extrapolation, the height of the cat was worked out to be less than two sides of breeze blocks high - in other words under eighteen inches high to the shoulder.

Over a very pleasant lunch, the editor agreed that he would no longer refer to the image as being of the "Beast", but would call it a large cat. That way, both parties were satisfied. He did not seem too distressed, as he had got mileage out of the picture, and all the royalties had gone to charity. I retracted my constructed image claim, and the Cornish Guardian stopped referring to their `cat` as the "Beast"`.

Although we had been proved right, in that the Guardian's image was not the "Beast", the paper continued to use it to illustrate reports of sightings of the "Beast" so the victory was somewhat empiric. That was until March 2000.

THE BEAST AND I

As any teacher involved in the teaching of science knows, March is the time of year when thoughts turn to hectic activities for `Science Week`. As a special Millennium treat, Chris and I decided it was an appropriate time to host a "Beast Conference". To say that the telephone receiver rang off the stand is an understatement; half the population of Devon and Cornwall wanted to attend the debate. There was one person who was desperate to talk to me, he had left messages all over the College, leaving his phone number and urging me to contact him immediately.

On Monday evenings I teach a night class. I had a little time while I ate my tea, so to help the half-hour pass, I phoned up the person who was so desperate to speak to me; a man whose' identity I feel honour bound to mask, and whom I shall call `Mr Angry`.

After a very brief introduction, Mr. Angry's first question was, who was debunking the image that the Cornish Guardian was using to illustrate their "Beast" stories. I explained that as I was the photographic expert it fell to me to debunk the images. I was nearly deafened by the yell of "Yessss" down the phone; apparently Mr. Angrys' next-door neighbour had been photographing Mr. Angry's Abyssinian cat, and was selling the pictures to the Cornish Guardian. We spent several minutes exchanging details, which would allow me to verify that image and its location matched those of the image used by the paper. In a word: Result!

It was with barely concealed glee that I asked the paper's receptionist to put me through to Mr. Cooper, the Cornish Guardian's editor. Mr. Cooper was not there, but his deputy editor Nick Knight was. To be fair to Nick, he did not interrupt as I listed all the facts. I knew about the location of the photographer, what he looked like and congratulated the paper on the papers' charitable contributions which took the form of royalties. Sufficient royalties, I informed him for the photographer to completely refurbished a fishing village's church roof! Never have the words that rhyme with "Clucking Bell" sounded so good to me. Unfortunately the Cornish Guardian continues to use the image and still takes the odd crack at me, but as the former Manchester Guardian - now the Guardian national newspaper - said in one of its reports: "When news is slack in the SW, they always resort to a "Beast" story!"

COULD THIS BE A RAT I SMELL

Early in July 1998 I was called into the Biology Laboratory, where I found Chris with two members of that honourable profession, the national press! I was ushered to a seat on the back bench, and the video player was switched on. I sat there with ever widening eyes: it was the worst home video of a pet cat I had ever seen.

It appears that as a result of our investigations, Chris and I were being used to check out the authenticity of the video before the paper went to press. What I had just watched was what someone was claiming to be footage of the "Beast of Bodmin". I must give Chris credit; he at least did not burst out laughing like me.

One week later, Chris invited me down to the staff room for a coffee. "You remember that video footage we saw the other week? Well, it is going to be shown at Newquay Zoo - at an exclusive launch - under the banner of conclusive video footage of the Beasts existence."

Fortunately for Chris, he was going on holiday the very day of the launch, so it fell to me to spoil Mike Thomas's ("the head of the zoo's") day. It was all ar-

ranged, I was to cover the event as the photographic consultant for the Centre for Fortean Zoology - run by one Jon Downes from Exeter. `Photographic consultant`. That sounds good - but is there any money in it? Unfortunately the answer was no, but it looks good on my C.V., and it would get me into the Press Conference.

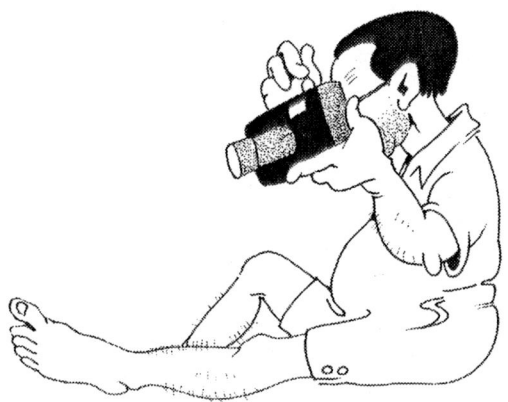

SKY'S THE LIMIT

So it was on the 21st July 1998 I filed the following report for the cryptozoology magazine "*Animals and Men*" – with the rider that it was to be read in an American accent.

"They say that the sun shines on the righteous. The problem - was the sun shining on Mike or me?

As I drove I had a smirk on my face, a smirk bigger than the one Sean Connery had as he watched Ursula Andress come out of the sea in *Dr No*. I was on a mission – I was a man with a question for Mike Thomas, and I knew the answer – because unbeknown to him I had already seen his video.

Two weeks earlier, as part of a team of `Beast-Busters` dubbed `Mr Pompous` and `Mr Arrogant` by the local press, I had seen his footage – footage which had somehow gotten into the hands of a national newspaper. These press boys were no mugs, they had seen other newspapers make fools of themselves and these boys weren't about to do the same, so they called in the `Beast Busters`. I am allegedly the photographic expert, and my partner Chris is the Biologist/Zoologist, but even I knew that Clive Lloyd did a better impression of an exotic cat as he walked to the crease for my beloved Lancashire, than the moggy we had watched. The clincher was, when the moggy walked past a forestry–style bench; it didn't even make the height of the horizontal beam.

As I drove on, one thought crossed my mind over and over again. Would he show the clip of the moggy with the bench? There were rumours that the tape had been re-edited. I knew if I had been him, I would sure as hell edit out the bench scene. There was another nagging question; was I going to see the *same* footage as we had been shown by the national newspaper?

11.30 am: Newquay Zoo, and the paving stones were cracking under the baking sun. I found myself and the rest of the press corps being ushered into - of all places - the Zoo's tropical house.

Mike began his five-act tragedy by showing us some fancy pictures of African Cats … mmmm not bad. This was followed by some plaster casts of impressive paw prints… getting better. He then introduced us to two kids Daniel and Kieran. They were `Beast Watch` …. Nice touch. Kids: the aah factor.

Next came Mike's rabbit from a hat, the anonymous photographer – `John`. Unfortunately the six–foot, blond haired John retold his story like a policeman giving evidence at the Old Bailey. Then the heat cracked the wrong man. John did not want to give the location of his video footage away – and then promptly revealed that the site was not a million miles away from the *Jamaica Inn* on Bodmin Moor.

Then came the moment we had all waited for – the video… all twenty seconds of it. To say that the silence was deafening is an understatement. The silence was broken by a female member of the press corps murmuring …. *"It's a cat!"* Mike was on the ropes, and beginning to look like a man going into his tenth round with Mike Tyson, but to give him credit, he still came out swinging. My sucker-punch about the missing footage was countered by the old anonymity strategy; Mike had forgotten that `Anonymous John` had already let the cat out of the bag over that one. The press sensed blood, and they were not about to let their prey loose. A voice called out: "All those who believe they have witnessed a video of a large cat please raise their hand. None were raised".

There then followed television interviews, analysis of the video. Remember the use of `Darky` by the BBC, which I mentioned in the introduction? Well here is where he fits into my story. By the time it came for me to leave, I was quite a popular chap. As I drove home one thought kept gnawing away in the back of my mind, "Why Mike why? It isn't even April Fool's day!" Then to cap it all it started raining, even the gods were weeping".

As Iwona and I watched my performance on television that night, somewhere in Italy a lady called Linda (one of the Colleges secretaries) had a very close encounter! Apparently she had returned to her holiday apartment and was having a clean-up when she was forced to run naked out of her shower to find out what I was doing in the lounge of her apartment. I, of course, was there but on the television, and unfortunately for her, the Italian men outside her apartment were more interested in her naked state than my broadcast!

I must confess that I felt somewhat upset about the way that Mike had been treated, so the following day I phoned him up and he agreed to talk to me, I filed the conversation in an article entitled *A chat with Lazarus*:-

"Twenty-four hours earlier I had participated in the ritual slaughter of Mike Thomas of Newquay Zoo, after a trial by media. There was one troubling thought

Zoological Gardens and British
Wildlife Rescue Centre

-press information-press information-press information-

Last February I was shown a short piece of film of a big black cat on Bodmin Moor.

On visiting the site we found some paw prints, which although not well defined, certainly encouraged further investigation.

The location was ideal territory - plenty of shrub and wooded cover, a still pond nearby. This particular area was also full of evidence of the habitats of field mice and voles - a good food source. As long as the food supply was good it was felt that the cat, or cats would return. Together with the person who had the first sighting we decided to keep watch.

Further sightings were made and my Assistant Curator, Matt Casey, actually saw it and verified the description as being at least 3 feet long seen from a distance. It was powerfully built, had a distinctive 'lope' to its movement and its tail was about 14 inches long with a rounded tip.

During the next few months several reports were made of black cat sightings within a ten miles radius, well within its feeding territory. Since such cats occupy a territory of some 30 miles or so other evidence became relevant and interesting. Paw prints found in South Cornwall became a vital part of the puzzle. These were big cat prints - no claw marks - unlike dogs, cats retract their claws.

Over the past two and a half years I have had sightings of large brown cats (Pumas), black cats (Panthers) and Lynx. It could also be possible that a species of black wildcats may exist and some of the gathered evidence at this location could verify this. The cat had large 'golden' eyes - a wildcat feature.

Mike Thomas
Newquay Zoo

18 July 1998

Newquay Zoo. Trenance Leisure Park
Newquay Cornwall. TR7 2LZ
Tel: 01637 873342 Fax: 01637 851318

MEMBER OF
THE FEDERATION
OF ZOOLOGICAL
GARDENS OF
GREAT BRITAIN
AND IRELAND

Is it or isn't it?

Beast of Bodmin – or just an ordinary moggy?

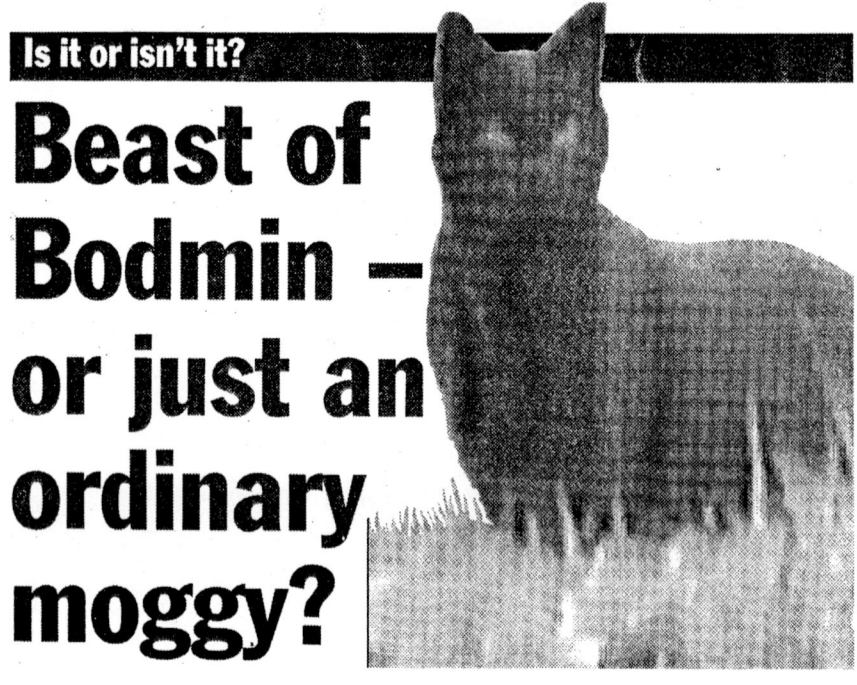

Video footage revives Beast of Bodmin debate

BY LUCIE MORRIS

GINGERLY TREADING across the grass is what appears to be a well-fed domestic black cat.

But according to experts the animal caught in "video evidence" unveiled yesterday is the infamous Beast of Bodmin, the puma-like creature blamed for killing scores of sheep and causing havoc across the West Country.

The debate about the existence of the Beast was revived again with the release of the footage of two big cats filmed on the Cornish wilderness.

The 20 seconds of video shot at a secret location by someone named only as "John", who lives on the moor, was shown at a news conference at Newquay Zoo yesterday.

The video shows one smaller "Beast" closely resembling a friendly feline and a larger 3ft 6in long black animal, walking out from behind some trees.

The video will form part of a dossier of evidence on the presence of big cats on and around the moor, which is to be submitted to the Government by North Cornwall MP Paul Tyler.

Reported sightings of large black cats and the deaths of scores of sheep and new-born calves stretch back a decade.

Mike Thomas, curator of Newquay Zoo and an expert on wild cats, who has been on the Beast's trail for the past three years, says the few seconds of video proves there are big cats roaming wild.

And he believes it could be a species of a kind of wild cat which was supposed to have become extinct in Britain nearly

The latest 'Bodmin Beast'

130 years ago. He said: "I believe this evidence shows a new species. Look at the rounded tail, look at the eyes – they are golden. Look at the power of the thing as it moves."

Mr Thomas also presented plaster casts and pictures of what he believes to be the Beast's paw prints. He has set up "Beast Watch", enlisting the help of local children to help him track down the elusive animal.

But Pat Crowther, a photography expert who attended the news conference, said he believed the video appearance of the "Beast" may have been the result of clever editing.

"Apparently the video is over fours hours long, there is one point when the cat walks towards a park bench and then the video is suddenly cut," he said.

However, Mr Thomas believes it is the "best evidence yet" of big cats in the wild.

The dossier will be sent to the countryside minister, Elliot Morley, together with details of around 60 other sightings gathered from around Cornwall over the past year.

●THE SURVIVORS: Mike Thomas (below) believes these two video pictures of large and powerful animals with golden eyes could prove once and for all existance of big cats breeding in the wild

Here Kitty Kitty............

rattling through my mind as I drank my evening scotch between James Bond style smirks. *Why, Mike? Why?*

I needed to talk to him, and I needed to talk to him fast. Surely a man of his intelligence would not put himself through such treatment deliberately! How could I talk to him? Would he talk to anyone? Was he capable of talking after what the BBC had done to him the previous evening?

In desperation I resorted to a modern mystic method of communication.... I used the telephone. Surprise! he would actually talk to me. Like an impatient kid in a toy shop begging for a toy before his parents dragged him outside again, I blurted out my question without giving him the chance to question my parenthood or cut me off : "Why? Mike Why? You must have realised that something like the murder of Caesar was going to take place at the press conference."

For a man who had been sacrificed by the media twenty-four hours earlier, his voice was clear and calm as he told me what *should* have happened the day before.

Originally there were to have been five members of the local press in attendance, by invitation only, and no, I had not been one of those invited. They were to view the video footage, and then have a "gentleman's discussion" about the footage, during which Mike would give his argument for the footage being that of a "wildcat" – not a "Beast", a puma, or a panther or any large man eating felid, as the public imagined the "Beast" to be. The results of this discussion were to be reported, and any fears that the public might have about a man/child/large pet-eating "Beast" would have been allayed.

"Wild cats are a fairly large animal and are definitely not in the habit of revealing themselves in public," I chipped in. "Not necessarily so" retorted the calm Mike, explaining that they are in fact no larger than a domestic cat. I believe this was his defence against my lack of park-bench footage the previous day. He continued – combine this urbanisation and perhaps the dietary needs of these animals and that might outweigh their fear of human contact.... Mmmmmmm!

Mike continued to outline his theories of wildcat population and urbanisation and hybrids, still in a cool, calm tone. "But Mike" I nearly screamed, "What was the reason for showing the video to the press like you did?"

The answer? "To show the general public what a wild cat looks like, and hopefully more members of the public would come forward with their sightings, photographs and video footage."

"But", I interrupted, "after seeing what happened to you, would you get in touch with you?"

The surprise is, it appears that Mike's gamble has worked. He said that he had received four phone calls in the previous few hours reporting sightings of a large

black cat terrorising the cat population in Liskeard, and his team were investigating the sightings as we spoke.

There was one point that we both agreed on. Until the general public sees either still images or video footage in any shape or form of large cats from Cornwall or Devon to the quality the public expects from wildlife programs and magazines, then the sceptics still have the upper hand.

Conclusion: Reports of the demise of Mike have been greatly exaggerated. As you read this he is probably on a "wild cat chase". If he comes up with the goods, I for one will back him. If however there are any doubts in my mind then...."

I had a strange encounter the night I filed this report. `Anonymous John` phoned me. This was quite remarkable, considering my phone number is ex-directory. John gave me about an hour of grief, on the theme of: `How dare I question his story`. John then said something quite remarkable. He wanted me to tell him what camera equipment he would need to get the definitive image of the "Beast". Oh, and money was no problem because he saw the "Beast" regularly, therefore the reward money was as good as in his pocket.

Being slightly miffed at the abuse I had suffered earlier in the conversation, I gave him a list of the most expensive equipment I could think of. Some camera shop must have thought it was Christmas when `Anonymous John` turned up with his shopping list. The sad part for John, despite his threats to insert cameras where the sun does not shine, and make his fortune from his "Beast" pictures, I have still to see a single image that he could have taken, and that's years after I first saw his video footage.

AN INSIDER'S VIEW OF THE "BEAST CONFERENCE"

My colleagues, my friends and, yes, even my family are all agreed on one thing – I am an egotist. Any opportunity to get my name in print or appear on television and I'll take it. I could end up looking a compete idiot, but it doesn't matter I'll still do it. There are drawbacks to fame however, after the Newquay Zoo incident I was called `Pat Crowther` in all the national newspapers. After having been interviewed by two journalists for a "lads" magazine, I was continually referred to as `Paul Crawford` throughout the article. Mind you, it could have something to do with the interview being conducted in a public house!

Because of this egotistical streak, certain people - including Chris - know that if I am involved in an event, then the degree of publicity generated tends to far exceed the global importance of the event.

In 2000 the opportunity to feature in a public debate, even if it is about exotic cats and "Beasts" was an opportunity too good to miss. Chris wound me up and pointed me in the right direction.

- THE BEAST AND I -

The weekend before the debate, Chris came down to St. Austell for a final briefing session over bottles of red wine and a large "spag bol". In an effort to incorporate a degree of learning into the event Chris had made some silhouettes of different cats made from plywood. These were to be incorporated into a display illustrating both domestic and exotic cats for identification purposes. As Iwona is the only true artist out of the triumvirate, it was left to her to paint the silhouettes while Chris and I refined our speeches.

At this point I have to introduce you to 'Tiger'. Tiger is the male cat in the Crowther household. Apart from being a tabby cat, Tiger can best be described as a Geordie. You may have seen the type on 'Match of the Day'; cheering on Newcastle United in the freezing cold, wearing only tight jeans and a white tee shirt with a packet of fags tucked under their sleeve. In a word they are 'hard', and by association Tiger is HARD!

Tiger has an awesome reputation in the closed world of St. Austell cats. Not only does he stomp rather than walk, not only will he attack his loving owners without the slightest provocation, but - and this is probably the main reason for his macho reputation - he survived an assassination attempt while he was fishing for koi. The proof - if any is needed - is that he did have to have a steel-hunting pellet removed from his spine. The operation was photographed and reported on in the *Plymouth Evening Herald*, and he does like bringing Koi Carp home for Iwona and I to pass on to colleagues who have ponds. Humans do not mess with this cat! Nor for that matter do other cats.

Back to the story. As the three of us were eating, Tiger shambled in through the cat flap and gave us a derisory meow before heading up stairs for a post excursion kip. As he rounded the door leading to the hall there was this almighty screech and hissing from him. The three of us rushed into the hall to find out what the commotion was. There was Tiger, fur all on end with a tail that Basil Brush would have been proud of, cowering from ... the cutout silhouette of the leopard! Iwona had left the cut out leaning against the wall to allow the paint to dry and Tiger had thought it was the real thing. It took us half an hour to calm Tiger down, after which we congratulated Iwona on the realistic paint job she had done on the silhouette.

In the week leading up to the event, Chris and I had arranged to be - and were - interviewed by almost every radio station in the land, and every local radio and television station in Devon and Cornwall. Those interviews that I could not do due to teaching commitments, Chris did and *vice versa*. Either together or separately we had been interviewed for just about every media outlet in the UK. People were trying to contact us for interviews or quotes from as far afield as Cardiff, Kent and Radio Ulster. Even more bizarrely they wanted to hear the thoughts of Messer's Crowther and Moiser on the "Beast of Bodmin" in

X-Files open on the beast

PAM GUYATT weighs the evidence and decides that she's never liked cats of any size anyway...

PAWSE for a while and consider the beast – the Beast of Bodmin, that is.

And possibly the Beast of Dartmoor, Exmoor, the South Hams, and anywhere else it – or they – pop up.

Sightings, blurry snapshots, video evidence, carcasses of dead sheep and residents and visitors prepared to swear blind they've seen something nasty, if not in the woodshed then heading sharpish over the hills and far away all contribute to the tail, sorry, tale of the beast.

It may be a big cat; black pumas seem to be the most likely explanation, abandoned to fend for themselves.

And they may be breeding in the West Country.

Who knows? If the Marines can't find them – and they've tried and failed – then probably nobody can.

However, a Plymouth evening on March 24 at 7.30pm, hopes to Scully the facts – or, in non-cult-speak, to cast the cold hard light of reason on

CAT'S CRADLE: Large puss or small predator, there's a debate to attend

To be held at the drama studio in the College of Further Education's Goschen Centre, King's Road, Devonport, the evening has four confirmed speakers already.

Paul Crowther, a photographic expert, will assess the photographic evidence produced so far.

John Downes, a cryptozoologist and director of the Centre for Fortean Zoology, will speak on Fortean (as in Times) aspects of cat sightings, possibly with something less than the aforementioned cold hard light of reason.

ogist as opposed to the crypto kind, will take on puma and leopard ecology and whether they could survive the climate of the South West (residents barely do, so how we expect pumas to, heaven only knows).

And Chris Moiser will examine the Dangerous Wild Animals Act of 1976 and inquire whether it was the cause of the beasts wandering in wild places, or merely the scapegoat.

Admission is free, but seating will be limited, so book now with Linda Baker on 305300.

Please note the date of the evening

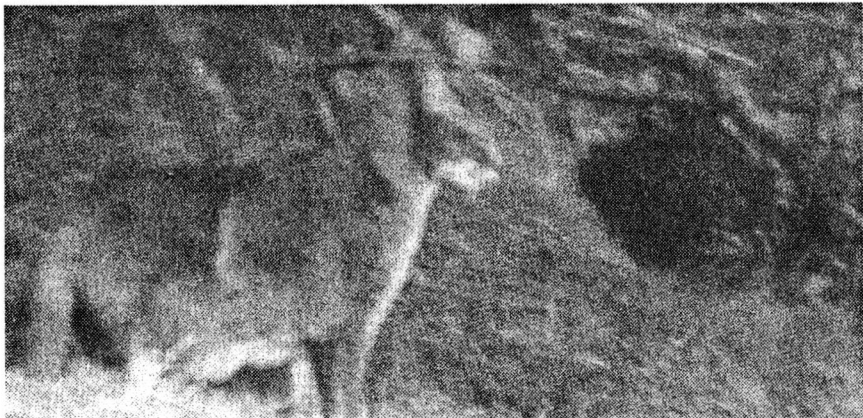

This exclusive picture of a puma-like animal taken by a Cornish Guardian reader near St Austell caused major national interest when it was published on our front page in November, 1997

This exclusive picture of a puma-like animal taken by a Cornish Guardian reader near St Austell caused major national interest when it was published on our front page in November, 1997.

Conference for big cat spotters

by IAN SHEPHERD

A MAJOR conference is to debate the existence of big cats roaming Cornwall and other parts of the West Country and organisers are on the prowl for people who might have seen the elusive creatures.

The conference is scheduled to take place at Plymouth College of Further Education on March 24 and will seek to separate fact from fiction on the issue. CFE photography lecturer Paul Crowther will examine photographic evidence and is anticipating a lively debate.

He said: "We want as much public participation in the debate as possible, particularly from people who have come face-to-face with big cats or have pictures or other evidence."

Over the past 10 years sightings of puma-like creatures have fuelled the debate. And a small but steady loss of livestock, particularly in North Cornwall, has been attributed by experts to classic "big cat" kills.

Among the speakers will be Mike Thomas of Newquay Zoo, CFE lecturer and cat expert Chris Moiser and Jonathan Downes, director of the Centre of Fortian Zoology.

The debate will be a highlight of Science, Engineering and Technology 2000 – a national college open day.

Mr Crowther said: "The problem we have had is finding people who will argue against the beast's existence. There have been so many sightings and reports it is hard to be sceptical."

North Cornwall MP Paul Tyler has made repeated calls for a new inquiry by MAFF into the existence of big cats roaming and breeding in the wild throughout his constituency. An earlier inquiry proved inconclusive.

"Not all the reported sightings can be wrong," said Mr Tyler. "And we must find a solution to the farm livestock that is regularly killed in classic big-cat style.

"MAFF must do a proper job of discovering what is out there."

■ *To book a place at the conference call Paul Crowther on 01752 305300.*

from: Paul Tyler CBE   MP for North Cornwall

HOUSE OF COMMONS
LONDON SW1A 0AA

Mr. Paul Crowther,
Dept of Science and Health,
Plymouth College of Further Education,
Goschen Centre,
Saltash Road,
Plymouth,
Devon, PL2 2BD.

Please quote ref : PT/MRS/1534

4 February 2000

Dear Mr. Crowther,

I was very interested to hear of your proposed evening of talks and discussions on March 24th.

As you will know, I've taken an active interest in this subject for many years, convened the conference at Bodmin in 1994 and have since (both inside and outside Parliament) maintained pressure to try and ensure that the information base for evidence of the "Beast" is responsibly handled.

I'm very sorry, therefore, that a prior engagement at the other end of my constituency prevents me from taking part in your discussion.

However, I must ask you to make one important correction. The good citizens of the town of Bodmin are naturally frustrated and fed up with being described as "beasts". To my knowledge there has never been a siting of a wild big cat in the town. The correct designation is "the Beast of Bodmin Moor". It would be equally silly to describe the Somerset version as the "Beast of Taunton".

I hope that you can make sure that this misrepresentation is corrected.

With best wishes
yours
Paul Tyler

PAUL TYLER

PLEASE: 1. Quote our reference on all correspondence.
2. Reply to: Constituency Office, Church Stile, Launceston, Cornwall PL15 8AT (01566 777123)

Chicago in the good old US of A.

I was so used to talking to newspaper journalists from all over the land, that I fell totally for the practical joke from my next-door neighbour who phoned me up purporting to be a reporter from the Scottish Herald. He asked if I knew anything about the "Beast of Glasgow"! I then went into this long ramble about not knowing about the reporter's "Beast" but.... I was finally brought to my senses by raucous laughter from the caller! This practical joke was - it seems - a direct result of my neighbour nearly crashing his car while he was driving to work. At a particularly tricky part of his journey, I had interrupted his radio listening in my capacity as an expert on the "Beast of Bodmin". Revenge was his.

To say that things were perhaps getting a little out of hand, can best be illustrated by a letter I received from one of the Cornish members of Parliament. The letter informed me that to the best of his knowledge no one had been attacked in the town of Bodmin, and so would I stop referring to the "Beast" as the "Beast of Bodmin", but use its full title: "The Beast of Bodmin Moor." That said, he did wish us luck with the debate, and hoped that the event would further the campaign for the "Beast" enquiry to be re-opened.

On the day of the debate, Chris and I were doing a check with the college receptionists about the number of people who were booked into the event, when an exceedingly attractive secretary called to Chris across the foyer. "Thanks for waking me up this morning", Chris did something I have seldom seen a grown man do – he blushed. It transpired that BBC Radio One had interviewed Chris, and they had broadcast the interview on the seven o'clock news bulletin, just as her radio alarm cut in.

Chris bolted for his nine o'clock lecture and left me holding the fort, a job I did manfully while smoking a pipe in the doorway of the college. The only time anyone gets to meet 'management' these days is when you are in trouble. Therefore it came as quite a shock when the deputy principal came up to me. I thought that he was going to complain that I was polluting the atmosphere with my pipe smoke. But no. He had sought me out because, he had - as he said - " put up with my dulcet tones" as he was sat in a traffic jam outside the college. Fortunately, he had managed not to stall the car as the report interviewing me for the debate came over the airways, but it had been a close thing, he informed me as he took long hard deep breaths of the smoke-laden air.

"Are you all right"? I enquired.

"Yes, I'm an ex smoker! Keep up the good work", and with a pat on the shoulder he was gone.

SOMEONE GET THAT BLOODY PHONE!

I spent the rest of the morning fielding telephone calls until six o'clock when it was time to set up the drama theatre for the debate. The line-up for the debate was quite impressive and each speaker was given ten minutes to put his or her arguments for or against the existence of the "Beast".

Jon Downes from the Centre for Fortean Zoology talked on the subject of myths and Man's need for such myths in the 21st Century. Ellis Daw - the owner of Dartmoor Wildlife Park - talked on exotic cat behaviour, and his experiences with pumas. Richard Freeman, a full-time cryptozoologist, reported on the incidents that he had been involved with, and enlightened the audience on the differences between the different types of kills he had seen. There was the Devon and Cornwall Police wildlife co-ordinating officer who reassured the audience that the police were not out to kill the "Beast", and informed them that there were in fact far more dangerous animals roaming the Devon and Cornwall countryside. Chris talked from a scientific standpoint, explaining how the existence of the "Beast" was not folklore, but based on scientific evidence. Most importantly, it is probable that the "Beast" is likely to become as urbanised as the fox, especially as Man builds more and more housing which is encroaching onto the

'Beast's' territory. It is fair to say that this was the comment of the night, and was duly reported in all the local papers and several of the national newspapers that had sent reporters.

Just what did I contribute to this discussion? Apart from publicly de-bunking the photographs of the Beast that have appeared in the press, I tried to persuade the audience that they were being conned into seeing what they wanted. I did this by illustrating my argument with photographs of the Loch Ness Monster—photographs which had proved to be fakes. I even tried to persuade the audience that man had not even left earth, let alone set foot on the moon, and all I got for my efforts were nods of agreement. To say that I was preaching to the converted is an understatement. So desperate were my efforts to provoke some reaction that I over ran by ten minutes and nobody - not even the master of ceremonies - brought me to order.

After two and a half-hours that turned into a consensus of opinion as opposed to the heated debate I had tried to instil, the proceedings were brought to a conclusion by the panel being asked if they believed in the 'Beast's' existence - to which there was a unanimous – "yes`', and being unanimous that included me. That was not quite the end of the evening: the speakers and some of the audience were then interviewed for the Carlton Television late night local news. It is amazing how the television cameras bring out the wannabe celebrity in people.

The following morning Chris and I were like a couple of actors devouring the stage press after a first night. We had every newspaper in the land spread over the coffee tables in the staff room. To say that our colleagues mocked us is putting it mildly – but then they don't have scrapbooks as full as ours!

FEMALE VICARS AND FARMERS (WELL IT MAKES A CHANGE FROM VICARS AND TARTS)

After the media circus generated by the "Beast Conference" had died down, the year that was 2000 petered out as a damp squib. "Beast" sightings were few and far between, and photographs of "beasts" and large cats were so absent as to be conspicuous. It could be have been said that `rain stopped sightings`.

There was however one interesting case reported in the *Cornish Guardian* involving a Farmer Vincent who had a few of his lamb stock mysteriously killed. As all good farmers do, Farmer Vincent reported the incident to MAFF who promptly sent the carcasses for autopsy. A month later, primarily because there had been no follow up reports in the Guardian I contacted the farm and spoke to Mrs Vincent.

It would appear that MAFF (later to be called DEFRA), were hedging their bets. The report from the autopsy agreed that a large unidentifiable animal had killed

the animals, but it was not prepared to speculate as to the species concerned.

I phoned the *Guardian* to inform them of the developments, but nothing was reported in the following week's paper. However two weeks later there was a report. It transpires that Farmer Vincent's neighbours had spotted several large dogs on the loose in the vicinity of the Vincent's farm, and the neighbours were of the opinion that the dogs had caused the deaths of the Vincent's stock, and the farmer tended to agree with his neighbours.

The year 2001 was something completely different. Firstly there was the sighting by the female vicar with a belief in God that defies belief. Well perhaps that is putting a little strongly, but the vicars' actions certainly defy belief - if what she reported is true, and who am I to doubt the word of a woman of the cloth? It appears that the vicar and her daughter were driving home one afternoon in the vicinity of a sightings hot spot, when they saw it! A very large black cat sat on a wall! The vicar stopped her car, and despite the desperate protestations of her daughter, the vicar got out to take a closer look. In the press report, the vicar said that the "large cat" was a puma, and that after a few seconds of watching the vicar, the puma disappeared over the wall. The vicar did however say that she very much regretted not having had her camera with her.

Now, I have beliefs that I hold very dear, but as stupid as I am, I for one would not get out of a car to go and get a closer look at an anomalous looking cat especially - like the Vicar - if I was aware of the existence of the "Beast". If the cat was - as the vicar said - a puma, then all I can say is that it is a good job that God *was* on her side, although if it were a puma as she says, then it would have been the puma's natural response to retreat from possible confrontation.

The next case goes to show how weird people are, and I must confess that I only heard the story from the people involved, or rather the people on the receiving end of the evidence. One of the problems of being regarded as an `expert`, is that people ask your advice and opinion on their material pertaining to the "Beast". Fortunately I get to look at pictorial evidence but others involved in the "hunt" for the "Beast" are less fortunate. The deputy editor of the *Cornish Guardian* Nick Knight, and Mike Thomas of Newquay Zoo were both unlucky enough to be presented the same piece of evidence, although Nick claims to have been the first recipient, and being unable to verify what he was looking at, he sent the man to Newquay Zoo to show Mike the evidence.

Mike was sat in his office, having - as he described it - a moments of quiet contemplation, when this person came in to his office saying something about having proof of the "Beast`s" existence, and started to wave this `thing` about under Mike`s nose saying "look at the print in the middle of this". What the man was waving about was in fact a not quite dried out "cowpat" with a dogs paw-print

WESTERN MORNING NEWS • TUESDAY JULY 21 1998

Beef farmers says animals' throats and chest cavities were torn away

Big cat blamed for slaughter of calves

● **WORRIED**: Farmer Martin Appleton (right) believes a big cat killed his calves and (above, with 10p piece for scale) one of the large paw prints

Minister to see 'beast' video

MICHAEL TAYLOR

TWO calves which both met violent deaths in the last few weeks may have been savaged by big cats.

Both calves owned by beef farmer Martin Appleton, of Bodwannick Manor Farm, Nanstallon, had their throats and chest cavities torn away.

One of them was dragged across the farmyard and later dug up after Mr Appleton had buried it.

Mr Appleton said yesterday that he would be very surprised if there was not some form of large wild cats in the area.

"Several people who have been out riding in the woods in the early morning say they have seen both a young black cat and an adult," he said.

The first calf, which was under medication, was killed about six weeks ago.

The other, a strong, healthy young calf, was found under a hedge near the farmhouse earlier this month.

in the middle of it. It must have been some event, because even though it was several weeks later that Mike reported the incident to me, he still seemed shocked that some one would carry a semi-dried out cowpat all the way around Cornwall, especially as in Mikes view it was so obviously a print of a dog.

While all this was going on, my friend Chris and I were being filmed for a Channel Five program entitled the `A-Z of Beasts`. The interviewer asked us the usual questions about the "Beast of Bodmin", which we answered with our usual enthusiasm. Once the interview was over we were asked if we knew anything about other "Beasts" on their list?

This was an opportunity too good to miss, after a knowing wink to Chris I said that we knew a certain amount about the Yeti and Bigfoot! Positions were re-established and the interviewer looked at me and said "Paul, what can you tell me about the Yeti and Bigfoot?" I looked at her in my most serious manner and without as much as a smirk said. "One is brown and shaggy, the other one is white and shaggy*, - the brown shaggy one has his own television series and is called Harry and he lives with the Henderson's..." and for good measure I added that there was "several thousand miles not to mention an ocean between them."

There is an odd coda to this event, when the program went out on air; the *Times* Newspaper listed the program in its "choice" section. However there was a sting in the tail, the piece advised viewers to watch the program as it was the best example of the poor television output that Channel Five was transmitting at that time. Talk about being damned with faint praise.

Vicar convinced she saw 'Beast' on Bodmin Moor

* EDITOR'S NOTE: Although media depictions, and especially cartoons, of the yeti often show it as being a white-furred ape-man, all eyewitness accounts refer to an ape - most probably an animal related to *Gigantopithecus blackii* of the Pleistocene - with shaggy reddish brown hair!

THE ZOOKEEPER'S REVENGE AND STRANGE BOXES?

It is said that time is a healer, but occasionally it takes time to get one's revenge, and this is one of those occasions where the virtue of patience certainly paid off. Mike Thomas and I are by now on very good terms. We even phone each other up to check out each other's opinion on the latest "Beast" news. When Newquay Zoo put itself in self-imposed closure due to the foot and mouth disease outbreak of 2001, it began losing somewhere in the region of £40,000 a week. So when it became financially suicidal to remain closed, it was a case of `all hands to the pumps`.

In an effort to boost the zoo's income a "Beast Week" was organised, so Chris and I made ourselves available. On the first weekend of the event, Chris and I stood in the pouring rain talking to anyone who was interested in the "Beast". While it could be argued that we did not do a great deal in terms of drawing in a great crowd of visitors to the Zoo, at least we feel that we attempted to help the situation. There was however a fresh piece of news – it is rumoured that there was a film involving the "Beast" about to be made, and Mike was gathering as much information as he could to supply it to the producers of the film. I was asked to bring the manuscript for "this" to contribute towards the background information for the film the following weekend, and while we were going to be at the Zoo could Chris and I deliver the feeding time talk to the public.

So one week later, Chris and I returned to deliver talks on the lions and pumas' respectively, while Iwona - for some mysterious reason - was asked to re-furbish the Tropical House.

The three of us arrived about lunch-time. We were armed with a few hundred weight of tropical plants, and a stack of Chris's books which I assume are still on sale in the zoo bookshop. While we were helping Iwona move the plants into their new home, I found myself being stalked by a rather burly man in a combat jacket. Eventually he gathered up enough courage to ask me where Mr Thomas's office was. After a little quizzing, I found that he had a plaster cast of a paw-print that he wanted to show to the "experts".

This was exactly what the "Beast" event had been devised for. Could we - despite having suffered in the cold - finally have proof of the "Beasts'" existence? I told the man to bring the print to the main office, and rounded up the others.

In moments of excitement I have been known to take a quick puff on my pipe to gain some composure, and this was one of these occasions. By the time I went into the office, the paw print had been unveiled, and was on general view on the desk. In my inimitable style I took a quick glance at the cast and declared: "It's a dog's".

Iwona grabbed me firmly by the lapel, and dragged me out of the office for another "smoke". It would appear that I had fulfilled my potential as a graduate of the `Margaret Thatcher/Prince Phillip School of Diplomacy`.

When it comes to `glaring at husbands`, I think Iwona set the world record for the longest glare ever given to a husband who has put his foot in it. I felt compelled to stand outside the office, while Mike and Chris tried to calm the owner of what turns out to have been a twelve-year-old plaster cast of a dogs paw print.

While the cast might well be that of a dog, it must be said that it must have been one hell of a big dog, as the paw print was the size of the span of my hand at rest, and I wear a size medium/large golf glove. Once the man had recovered from the brutally frank disappointment of my instantaneous evaluation of his cast, Mike and Chris persuaded him to leave the cast in a locked glass case for evaluation by the public.

BIG CAT WEEK at NEWQUAY ZOO

Saturday MARCH 24th to Sunday APRIL 1st

BIG CATS IN THE WILD IN BRITAIN, FACT OR FICTION

Come and see the evidence and talk to the investigation experts.
VIDEO INFORMATION, PAW PRINTS, PHOTOGRAPHS and **BIG CAT TRAILS**.
If you have any information of 'The Beast of Bodmin' come and talk to us.

DON'T MISS IT

Regular talks and trails.
Normal Zoo admission price.
Telephone : 01637 873342

I must say that Chris placed the cast in the case with all the dignity he could muster. I feel that I can go as far as to say, that if it had been a funeral, there would not have been a dry eye in the congregation, as the cast was placed in the most prominent position, and the lid slowly lowered and locked.

After the ceremonial positioning of the cast it was feeding time for the "big cats" and the "expert's" performances. Chris was first up talking about lions! However, I don't think that the quite substantial crowd gleaned that much information. Every time Chris spoke, the crowd's ears were bombarded with feedback. He was later to blame the drizzle, which was falling fast, for the slight technical problems he encountered.

Next, after a big build up by Mike, it was me talking on Pumas. Mike had been kind enough to supply me with a list of the cat's names and that was it. The microphone was in my hand, and Mike was standing - arms folded - in front of me with an expression of smug contentment on his face.

It is at times like this that the family motto of those Crowthers in my family living in Cornwall comes into play: *Proper preparation prevents piss-poor performances.* What Mike had *not* noticed, was that I was standing behind the crowd as they watched the cats being fed, and I was reading his information boards as the event unfolded. Not only did I supply valuable information about their habitat, feeding routines etc. but I then started to tell the crowd how profitable faking images of the `beast` was. This part of the talk at least got a large number of the crowd to turn and face me. Predictably this caused me to then waffle on a little too long, but my performance was not *that* bad. I would give myself 7/10, although Iwona said the talk was more a victory of style over substance.

Throughout the first quarter of the year there were several more sightings. However while in discussion with my peers I formulated a simple proposition, which should cut down on the amount of time, we spend chasing dead ends.

If a person claims to see their "Beast" continually over a period of time greater than four days, then I believe that we can discount the sighting because wild cats generally do not feed in one area for longer than three days. Wild cats tend to `farm` their prey, that's why they have extensive territories.

The second quarter of the year began with a bang; there on the screen and in the newspapers was the amazing story of Lara…

"LARA"
THE LYNX OF LONDON TOWN

Although on first glance the capture of a Lynx in Golders Green, London has little to do with the "Beast of Bodmin", this is an observational conundrum.

It is now a fairly well documented fact that `Lara the Lynx` was captured in London. What is not so well known is that there are several versions of the event. The national newspapers ran reports of the story on Tuesday the 8th May 2001, the BBC and ITV ran the story on their text facilities twenty-four hours earlier. This is easily explained because the Monday was a Bank Holiday. What is not easy to explain, is that each source gave a different location for the actual capture of the Lynx. Cricklewood was one site and Golders Green was another. Even more perturbing to someone trying to work out the truth behind the story, is that the Lynx was actually caught on Friday 4th May 2001.

The actual location in this case is not the important factor. After scouring all the available sources of information on the captured Lynx, the following facts emerged. The Lynx was female, about eighteen months old, and had a slightly damaged left hind leg. She was slightly emaciated, but otherwise in good condi-

tion. The cat was sat on a back wall when it was reported to the authorities, and by the time the authorities arrived, it was hiding under a shrub in the garden (enclosed by the wall on which it was first observed). The RSPCA and London Zoo took two attempts to dart the poor cat. After being jabbed in the backside once Lara took off. The officials commenting on the event said that it was by sheer chance that there had been no students playing in the sports field that the cat escaped through. The suggestion being that the cat was a potential danger to humans!

I immediately contacted Mike Thomas at Newquay Zoo to consult on the available evidence. After half an hour we both agreed the following: The Lynx was an illegal pet - it had to be, as no one had claimed it, or informed the relevant authorities of its escape. It may have been involved in a slight road accident - hence the damaged leg - but of most interest was the animal's behaviour.

The cat had been sitting on the garden wall as if waiting to be fed, and furthermore it stayed in the garden still anticipating being fed after a period of time. The report said that the Lynx was in good condition except for being slight emaciated, therefore Mike and I concluded, the Lynx had escaped or been released no more than five days earlier. This leads us to believe that the Lynx was heavily reliant on a person to feed it, because there must have been food that was easily scavenged from bins, which would have been the Lynx's natural course of action if it was a genuine wild cat.

The net result is that there was a Lynx of unknown origin - very probably an illegal import or worse an `under the counter` sale. Mike and I proposed to anyone who would listen that the Lynx should be DNA fingerprinted. DNA fingerprinting would identify the origin of the Lynx in terms of place of birth, and its parentage. If it was an `under the counter sale`, then the repercussions for the Zoo or registered private owner of the parents, would be catastrophic in the extreme.

As interesting as it is going into the Lynx's background, there is one very important question left unanswered. Why did it take so long for anyone to report seeing it? The idea that a Lynx could roam around London for approximately five days without anyone noticing it beggars belief! If a Lynx can roam around London for five days without being detected by the numerous people who live and work in that area of London, who is to deny that a similar exotic cat can not survive and go unnoticed on Bodmin Moor for years!

To add to the mystery, there had been no further official coverage of the story from the press, London Zoo were keeping very quiet on the subject. Just where did the Lynx come from and what were the "officials" doing to trace the origins of it?

Beast of Cricklewood

Paul and Michaela Strachan

A phone call to the press office at London Zoo did not throw much light on the situation, although they did say that the staff had similar feelings over the treatment and housing of Lara, i.e. they were fairly sure that she was a very domesticated Lynx. As for tracing the origins of the cat, the Zoo said that was a RSPCA/Police matter, but no one had taken DNA samples. However the zoo was under the impression that the Police were in the process of acting on a tip off. So there could be more to report at a later date.

The story of Lara mysteriously died a death. No matter how hard I probed, the less I found out. No-one was talking. At this point I could speculate as to Lara's' original owners, but that would probably land me in trouble so I will leave that conundrum to those of you who believe in conspiracy theories.

May 2001 was one of those times when you have to pinch yourself just to check that you are living in the real world. Not only was Lara sitting in London Zoo, but suddenly the only thing that the world was interested in were fake images of the unexplained.

The first people to call on my alleged expertise as an image debunker were the BBC. They wanted me to do an interview with the distractingly beautiful Michaela Strachen for the BBC's *Countryfile* program. I must confess I put on a pretty awful performance; the reason for my poor performance was that I could not use the images that I had debunked in the press because of copyright restrictions. In the end I played around with some Zoo pictures by removing bars and chain fences. The presentation I gave was patchy to say the least. But the program that was transmitted was phenomenal; I actually looked and acted as if I knew what I was talking about. Thank you very much, BBC.

This was then followed by a spate of photographic magazines showing how to recreate classic fake images of the unexplained. The articles opened up with the usual UFO images using a Frisbee; a man dressed in a gorilla suit pretending to be "Bigfoot", and finally they produced an impressive fake of the Lough Ness Monster. The article was finished with a request for image fakers to come foreword to explain the how's, the what's and the wherefore's of their fake image (s). I wrote to them chiding them over their lack of a "Beast of Bodmin Moor" image. Then blow me down, in the *Sunday Mail* of the 27th May there was a double page spread of "new" Loch Ness Monster pictures taken by James Grey! I am beginning to think life is imitating art! Not only that, I won a camera bag for my "Beast" letter, so now not only can you get money for taking images of the "Beast", but you can get rewards for writing about the "Beast" as well. Will wonders never cease?

Just when it can't get any weirder, it does. Twice in one day. First was a phone call from Chris to inform me that we were required to give information on what

would be our third television program of the year, then, at a barbecue, I was informed that a big cat had been sighted some five years after the first reported sighting of it, in a location on the outskirts of St Austell.

I slept on the previous day's events, and woke up the following morning, having concluded that - as it had not rained in St Austell for over a week and the sun would have dried out the ground it was impossible to go gathering foot prints or evidence - so it would be the sightee's word against whoever's. Seeing as the sightee had been on safari several times, who was I to doubt her word? I spoke to Mike Thomas about the sighting, and from the background information we had on the lady, we decided that we had to take her word for it, and file the sighting as a possible.

TWO YOKELS GO TO WONDERLAND AND ONE HAS AN ULTERIOR MOTIVE FOR GOING (2002)

Headache tablets and sunglasses were like rocking horse dirt at Mrs Tregansers village shop during the third week of October this year. There was nothing conspiratorial or Fortean about this, it was just that the whole village had gone on a three-day drinking spree when I had accidentally revealed to Mr Tregale Sr. - the butcher - that my wife, Iwona, had been short-listed for an International `Technician of the Year` Award.

In our village, if "George the Dipso" as opposed to "Drunken Tresillian" cuts his grass, the whole village rushes to the pub and celebrates with at least four pints of *Brewers Armpit* from the microbrewery at the back of the pub. So, the prospects of one of the villagers winning a legitimate major industrial scientific award, was genuine reason to celebrate. Unfortunately there were problems; the presentation was to be held in London! When I say problems, I must say that one problem is relative. For me it was an opportunity, an opportunity to visit the "Beast of Cricklewood"!

We live in the middle of the most inaccessible county in England – Cornwall. Things happen at a pace in Cornwall that makes *mañana* seem quick. This is perhaps best illustrated by the fact that we have a five-figure telephone number, when everyone else in the country has six! So you can appreciate that going to

London was a scary proposition. To add to our feeling of trepidation, I had been asked to re-submit photographs of Iwona at work - in colour! Can you imagine how long it took to find a colour film in Cornwall? It is difficult enough to find 35mm film, let alone this new-fangled colour stuff.

The most important thing about living in a small community, is that if one of us has a problem then everyone has a problem. You bet I had a problem. That of the "Black Tie". Fortunately for me, Arthur the local undertaker and coal merchant promised me that he could arrange for `Thunder` to be re-shoed while we were in London. This meant that I could borrow his suit—minus the top hat of course. (Thunder I must inform you, is the four-legged, hay-eating propulsion unit used by Arthur to deliver both the dearly departed and the coal around the village).

That was me just about sorted. All I needed now was a bow-tie and a belt, as I am as stout as I am, but I am nowhere near as large as Arthur, so I needed a black belt if the trousers were to stay around my middle and not my ankles.

A meeting was convened in the pub, and the chaps all agreed that there was no way that I could go to London for the presentation using bailing-twine to hold up my trousers, even if it had been painted black to match the suit. There were visible shudders when `Drunken Tresillian` warned me what Iwona would do to me if I even thought of pulling such a stunt.

Things were looking bad when Claire Penhallurick - the barmaid - interrupted our heavy mumbling. "You know, I like to keep souvenirs to remind me of my lovers". She said. (We didn't, but that might explain where `Trembling Tresillian's` shirts kept disappearing to, and it might also explain why he trembled so much!). We just looked at her. "Well Paul, you can have these", she said dangling a belt and bow tie provocatively. "It'll cost you mind," and with that she grabbed me round the neck, and tried to suck the life out of me.

When I eventually was allowed to breath again, the pub was in uproar, and yet another four rounds of drinks were consumed in celebration of my acquiring a belt and bow tie. Well that was me sorted for the big day - but what about Iwona?

Full of the joys of spring, I arrived home brandishing my belt and tie. Iwona was not too impressed, and informed me that in an effort to prepare ourselves for the trip to `Wonderland`, we should visit the metropolis - Truro. Apparently old Mrs Pengelly had told her that she had read somewhere that there was this shop in Truro called S&M which she thought the paper said was the housewives choice for shopping in. The following Saturday, Iwona and I set off in our Sunday best to visit the big metropolis.

What a place Truro is. There are shops in Truro that are bigger than Mrs Tregansers' shop in the village. There are even shops that sell women's thingies (I didn't go in 'em cos I was too embarrassed). Eventually we found this shop called M&S. It was the biggest shop I had ever seen in my whole life. Iwona got very excited the closer we got to it. Obviously this was the shop that old Mrs Pengelly had meant, and not S&M, the shop we had found earlier. I must confess that on a personal note I did find myself getting more excited looking through the window of the S&M shop, especially compared to my emotions when looking in the windows of the M&S shop.

For some unexplainable reason, I just could not summon the willpower to go into the shops Iwona wanted to go into. What I saw in the shops Iwona liked was doing a better job of converting me to Christianity than the Reverend Trevaskus back at the village church.

It had been a very scary time for both of us out in the big metropolis, but we had managed to get her a dress, shoes and certain woman's' "things", and we even managed to buy all these things in less than four hours! Quite frankly the fellows in the pub did not believe me when I told them about the women's "things", and as for doing all that shopping in less than four hours including shopping for shoes, well they were quite incredulous! As a result of my report on the pre-adventure, the chaps tried to ban me for a month from the pub for telling such tall-tales.

Fortunately `Arthur the Undertaker` was on hand to assure them that such woman's "things" did exist, but even he was dubious about the length of time it took to buy all the wife's things. But, being a wise man, Arthur did point out to the assembled crowd that my wife was going to London because she had been short-listed for a science award. Therefore it might just be possible for a woman of her undoubted ability to do all that shopping in less than four hours.

Arthur - the village sage - is not only the undertaker and coalman; he is the most cosmopolitan person in the village. He had been born in East Taphouse; and in his youth he had ventured far enough into the world to discover West Taphouse, and there he found this lass called Demelza and married her. This also made Arthur the bravest man in the village.

Until Arthur had gone on his adventure, no man had ventured beyond the duck pond at the end of the village. Apparently there had been over sixty cricket balls lying in the verge just beyond the pond, but no-one had ever had the courage to fetch them, until Arthur had returned from his journey. Arthurs bride, Demelza, was another revelation to the villagers. Until Arthur's return all the men in the village believed it was normal for their wives to have Cauliflower eyes!

Well the day of the great adventure arrived, and the village turned out to see us

off from the train station. The sun was rising over the remnants of Tom's burnt-out barn which haven't been rebuilt in seven years, as the train pulled out of the station. We had been given pasties to remind us of our friends, and fortify us if we ran into strife, or any hazards on our great adventure.

Iwona and I were two hours into our adventure when the first stress-inducing event presented itself – the track was closed due to flooding. I panicked, but Iwona kept calm (she wasn't being nominated for this award for nothing), and clutching the pasties, we were transferred onto a bus and resumed our journey. Then after an hours' journey we were herded back on to another train. It took us a further four hours until we reached London.

At exactly the same time as we stepped off the train in London, we were greeted by the biggest clap of thunder we had heard since the big thunder-clap of '89. Iwona looked very scared as we suddenly found ourselves surrounded by thousands of people running here there and everywhere. Apparently the clap of thunder had set the fire alarm off in `the underground` (whatever that is), and the result was all these people rushing up to the surface. It was just like watching the rats run out of old Toms' barn when it caught fire on fireworks night.

Even outside of the station, there were people everywhere. We had never seen so many people in one place, not even at Great Granny Treganser's wake, and it is written down that over sixty people turned up for Great Granny Treganser's wake.

The people in London are very peculiar; it must be because London has so many buildings, and is so crowded that the people cannot have pets. Instead the people in London have cases on leads. Everywhere we looked there were people pulling their pet case! Now this is a sight you don't see in Cornwall!

Then there were the taxies. Gosh, all the black taxies in the world must live in London, cos we don't have 'em down in Cornwall. After queing for half an hour, we climbed into a taxi and asked him to drive us to our hotel. The response to our request by the taxi driver was a bit odd; he said it would have been quicker if we had walked to the hotel. He did seem rather surprised when we responded with the query, "How could we walk to the hotel if we didn't know where it was"?

The hotel was a funny place, this was the first one we had visited which had the "bouncer" behind a desk, Iwona pointed out that for a bouncer he talked in a very posh voice, and was a little lightweight, although his suit and tie made him look very smart.

We decided to eat the pasty as soon as we got into the room. We ate it in seclusion was because we had heard all sorts of things about food in London. To the

front of our thoughts were reports that they served their food naked, (that's the food that's naked not the people serving it) in London. The idea of seeing people eat food that didn't have pastry wrapped around it was a little daunting to say the least.

Seeing that Iwona was sufficiently fortified thanks to the pasty, I broached the subject of my ulterior motive for accompanying her. "Can we go to London Zoo", I enquired. Much to my surprise she agreed, provided that we used the underground, because she wanted to see were all those people had come from when the thunderclap had gone off.

Following the written instructions given to us by the "Bouncer" behind the reception desk, we managed to find the underground station. Iwona fed the ticket machine with all my change, and pressed the green button and much to our surprise the tickets came out - although she was upset that the machine didn't have a "nudge" facility on it. We stood on the platform for all of ten minutes, when - just as the "Bouncer" had predicted - the train arrived, and we got on.

At the next station, two very tall men of Jamaican extraction got on and sat opposite us. It didn't take long for the one with the gold tooth, the multiple earrings and the tattoo, which expressed his love for his mother, to enquire as what I was looking at. I explained that where we came from you didn't see people dressed in full basketball regalia walking down the street, let alone sitting on a train and apologised. By the time the basketball-playing duo had informed us that it was time to get off at our stop, we were getting on like a house on fire.

I had told a minor 'porky' by saying we were from Plymouth, and followed this by enquiring if *Plymouth Raiders* basketball team were any good? Well, that was it. If ever I had picked the right subject to talk to strangers about this was it. Not only did they give me the low down on Plymouth's basketball team, but as a bonus we where regaled with the duos sexual encounter in and on Plymouth's Union Street. Iwona and I both came to the conclusion that an away fixture against *Plymouth Raiders* was the number one fixture on their list, although Iwona had to apologise when my teaching hat accidentally landed on my head, as I reminded the gentlemen that as an educator I felt it was my duty to remind them to practice safe sex.

With the duo's best wishes for Iwona at the presentations ringing in our ears, we headed for the Zoo. Being a romantic at heart, the first thing I did was buy the wife an ice-cream. There is one thing about wives, and that is they can see through husbands as if they were made of glass. "I think we should head this way" she said as she led me by the hand to the Lynx enclosure. "Excuse Me," she said as she stopped a passing Zookeeper: "Which one is Lara"?

The keeper pointed to a lynx positioned just outside the main grouping. The

keeper went on to assure us that Lara was doing fine and that her leg had healed up. He didn't think that she had received her injuries in a collision with a car, but they could have been received as a result of her having jumped over a fence or some similar obstacle. She was eating well, but considering that she might not have eaten that much during her week of freedom, the amount of food she was consuming was about right. However it would take just a little longer for her to integrate fully into the group. When I questioned him as to his thoughts on Lara's origins, especially as she was so young, the keeper clammed up, and rapidly preceded on his rounds.

Having satisfied myself that Lara was in safe hands I set about photographing the world famous "Beast of Cricklewood" from as many different angles as it is possible to. Mind you, coming up with unusual compositions of a Lynx behind bars, tests even the greatest photographers. Iwona and I discussed the future for Lara, and came to the conclusion that she would probably have a long life at the Zoo - albeit an anonymous one - due to the secrecy that was still veiling her discovery and arrival at the Zoo. Iwona and I went for a stroll around the rest of the Zoo while throwing the appropriate food at the various birds wandering around the grounds. Who said that men can't multi-task?

With an hour and a half to go before the presentations, we had returned to the Hotel and were getting ourselves ready for the evening ahead without further adventure except for several laddered pairs of tights and the associated histrionics that follow such an occurrence.

Now I know that Iwona can juggle Winchesters full of fuming Sulphuric Acid while walking over hot coals. I know this, because I have seen her do this numerous times as glorified deities other wise known a `Lecturers` ask her for minor miracles of scientific preparation at short notice. But laddered tights! After being accused of being a "chocolate teapot" for the umpteenth time, I did what I would recommend to every man who find himself in a similar situation – I went outside for a smoke – I ran away.

At seven o'clock, an exceedingly elegant and composed Iwona plus myself got in a taxi and set off to the Dorchester Hotel for the presentation. On the way there we saw an astonishing sight, I don't mean the ones pointed out to us by out taxi driver/self-imposed travel guide. It seemed as though all the men in London dress just like James Bond - either that or every other man in London is a Bouncer. But something was not quite right. The men kept putting these brown bags to their mouth. Iwona and I looked at each other with raised eyebrows. Maybe all the men in London are like "George the Dipso" back home! Iwona and I exchanged silent nods as if to say, (and I do originally hail from Lancashire), *"there is now't as queer as folk"!*

We arrived at the event and having been announced we were introduced to these

men called David and Andrew, who kept plying Iwona with Champagne and insisting that they had their photograph taken with her. Unfortunately for David and Andrew, they did not know that Iwona is the only person to drink "Scrumpy Tom" under the table in the annual "last man standing" contest held every September in the Pub! I am afraid that David and Andrew were not that stable on their feet as they attempted to make their way to eat. In fact, if I am not mistaken, I am sure I saw Andrew rush out of the room halfway through the meal. That will teach them to mess with our Iwona!

I accompanied Iwona into the Ballroom to eat. I can confirm to you the rumours were right. They do serve food, which has not been wrapped in pastry, and boy did it taste good. To further confuse us, there were more knives at each place setting than there are in Bobs' fishing tackle shop! Fortunately, we both remembered Arthur's parting advice: "Start on the outside and work your way in!"

Unfortunately following Arthur's additional advice of: "always eat when you can because you never know were the next meal might come", Iwona and I had eaten all the contents of those little pots on the tables where we had drank the champagne. So we were - without putting too fine a point on it - stuffed before we even sat down to eat.

After the meal, this man from some television station I had never heard of, stood up and announced that the presentations would commence after every one who needed to had gone to the "Looe". I shrugged my shoulders at a very puzzled wife who whispered in my ear: "Why would they want to go to Cornwall at that time of night"?

The presentations started, and we were very surprised (why I don't know), to discover that the other guests on the table had also been nominated for awards. I suppose that was why they were there. As each category was announced, a photograph of the nominees was shown, and as each image was projected Iwona pointed at our fellow guests and yelled, "That's you"! I must confess that the pictures they use in London were more realistic than the picture shows we have in the pub. This usually comprises of `Drunken Tresillian` casting shadows with bits of his body yelling: "Guess what that is, my lover!!!" and shouting at the women: "It's bigger in real life", every time he does his shadow impression of an elephant!

Then it was time for the award for `Technician of the Year`. The compère read out the nominations, then he listed all the different activities they do. Then it was Iwona's turn; The man listed all the scientific things the wife did, and then disaster. He said "and next week she was going to wear her underwear over her trousers and saving the world". The wife looked at me in total panic. How the heck did he know about her super hero status? I just shrugged my shoulders, and suggested that maybe he had had the "Super Techie Brekkie". A Techie Brekkie

is a culinary delight that the villagers had named after my wife when she solved the great potential flood disaster of '99. Fortunately for the village, Iwona had had the foresight to remove the leaves covering the storm drain two hours before it started to rain, and so had saved the village from certain disaster.

Iwona did not win the award, which deservedly went to a virologist who had been locked in a laboratory for fifteen years. (Anyone who has been locked in a laboratory with smelly bugs for that long surely deserved to win something). But she was pleased that she had retained her anonymity as "Super Tec". (I think every one else in the room had consumed a little too much alcohol to notice the compéres revelation). We had a great night, which just got better the longer it went on.

At about three o'clock in the morning we went for a walk, and discovered a shop that sold these meaty things in a bun. We had stumbled across the reason that all those wannabe James Bonds kept putting bags to their mouths. They weren't drinking - they were eating! We explained to the person behind the counter, who insisted that she was really a social scientist carrying out research, that we needed extra bags so that "George the Dipso" could drink his wine while pretending to be a Londoner eating his meaty bun. We had to keep the lady happy, so we filled in the questionnaire and in exchange she gave us six bags for George.

We arrived back in the village just in time for the rush to the pub for the annual one-dart competition without any further mishap or distraction. We received the biggest welcome since Arthur had returned to the village with his foreign wife. Joshua the village crier, climbed onto the bar, and announced that in recognition of my wife's achievement in making the short-list for the award, she and I had been granted the honour of free drinks in the pub on any month that has a W in it.

`George the Dipso`, I am pleased to report, has written off to some Scottish chaps who are apparently based in America asking them to sponsor his drinking habit. After all, as he pointed out in the letter he got me to write, (this is not to besmirch George and his writing abilities, it is just that his DT's make holding a pen a very arduous task, so it is better all round that he gets someone to write his letters for him), George is advertising their product by hiding his bottles of wine in their logo-infested paper bag. Every time he has a surreptitious swig while walking around the village, he reveals their name and brand logo to the world, so why wouldn't they sponsor him.

Who says the people of Cornwall are slow?

The name is Crowther...
...Paul Crowther

TO WONDERLAND AND BACK AGAIN: THE CONTINUING STORY OF TWO YOKELS (2003)

Life in our little Cornish village was proceeding as usual, the sun was shining as I called into the local for a pint of Brewers Armpit, when I was accosted by "Mad Janet", the mother of Claire Penhallurick the bar maid.

"Eeeer" she screeched as she poked me in the guts. "You be goin to Londern again". I just looked suspiciously at her as she explained that she had heard that I was borrowing Arthur the undertaker's suit again. She continued by saying "You will meet someone called Sam, who would be accompanied by willowy maidens, I see you talking to people who talked in strange tongues from a distant land and you will also meet a Sponsor and see a Watcher and what you are looking for will be gone". With a "Stop reading Tolkein Janet", I completely forgot about having a pint and headed home instead.

Although the journey home is all of fifty yards, it is surprising how many thoughts you can cram into such a short journey. First there was the prospect of receiving old Mrs Pengelly's cheese, broccoli and tomato sauce pasties, then there were the evil thoughts about whether it was possible for an undertaker to bury himself, because that is what Arthur would have to do for telling Mad Janet about me borrowing his suit.

The following morning the village assembled at the train station, and after the presentation of the pasties to ward off evil on our journey, and having to kiss every female goodbye, and Iwona doing like wise to the male population of the village, we set off for London with the best wishes of the village ringing in our ears.

We were fully prepared for an eventful journey, but nothing happened. I read my magazines, and the paper. Iwona listened to her CD's; the journey was quiet no the journey was boring so much for `Mad Janet's` predictions.

After we had booked into the hotel, I went for a smoke outside. While I was contemplating nothing in particular, I was approached by a very large man in a tracksuit asking for a light for his cigarette. The man spoke in very broken English with a heavy East European accent. It turned out he was one of the coaches for *Dynamo Kiev* - the Ukrainian football team. The Kiev team was in London to play *Arsenal* the following night. Soon there was a minor crowd gathered around me - all talking in different languages - but unified by the common language of football.

Suddenly they all went away, when I told them I was a Liverpool fan (Dynamo do not have a very good record against `The Pool`). Surprisingly, one of them ran back towards me, and offered me his watch in exchange for my trousers! I hastily explained that as these were the only pair I had, unfortunately, I could not accept his generous offer. Perhaps Mad Janet's prophecy was coming true; after all I had met men from a distant land speaking in strange tongues.

"What did he want?" Iwona asked as she appeared beside me as if by magic. I explained what had happened, as Iwona took me by the arm. "Where are we going?" I enquired, as Iwona attempted to put a coat on me. "The Zoo". I did not need a second invitation as I pushed my arms through the last sleeve; I started to drag her behind me as we raced for the tube station.

This time there were no Jamaicans. In fact the train was empty when we got on it, and it was still empty at the time we got off. Iwona paid for the Zoo tickets and I got the ice cream. It didn't take us long to reach the Lynx enclosure. We both looked at the enclosure and at each other several times. Now I could not swear that I could identify Lara - the "Beast of Cricklewood" - but something was not right.

I accosted a zookeeper and asked if he could point out Lara - the "Beast of Cricklewood". "Oh she's gone to France", was the response.

The keeper was not too impressed by my interrogation of him, as he kept citing the alleged fact that he was `new` for his inability to answer my growing list of questions. He could not tell me exactly why Lara had been bundled off to

France, but he offered vague reasons which revolved around Lara's breeding and suitability, as she would be able to dilute the gene pool.

He got even more agitated when I pointed out that the Zoo did not know about Laras breeding capability, unless the Zoo had identified where Lara had come from, and if the Zoo did know where she came from, then they must have *some* idea who had owned her before she was found wandering around Cricklewood. If they knew this information, then surely the police had been notified, and some sort of prosecution has - or shortly would - be taking place, because she had been found wandering. Therefore I pointed out there were one or two potential prosecutions for the police to follow up on: One being the illegal importation of an animal classified under the Dangerous Wild Animals Act. If they didn't get a prosecution from that line of inquiries, then Lara had been owned legally and the prosecution would be for housing a Dangerous Wild Animal in inappropriate conditions, or in conditions which weren't suitable for the job they were intended to do.

To say the keeper was rattled would be an understatement, but he stuck to his line about being new to the job and not being able to help me. He even came up with the classic: "They are all in a meeting", when I asked if there was anyone who could answer my questions.

Iwona pulled me away from the keeper, as I continued to bombard him with questions about Lara. "Remember", she said "Lara is safe and that is something". I just remembered Mad Janet - something I was looking for had gone. I shoved my hands deep into my pockets, and kicked a stone up the path. How many more of Janet's predictions were going to come true? I wondered as we travelled back to the hotel.

At the Dorchester things could not have gone better. This time we were quite prepared for the undressed food, we found ourselves advising the others on the table to start on the outside, and work your way in when it came to the array of knives and forks, and Iwona managed to curtail her consumption of Champagne to only the one Magnum.

Iwona won the award for "Best Technician". She was so surprised, that I had to give her a nudge to get up and collect the award from the compére who was the same Channel 5 baseball commentator as the previous year. Being the polite person she is, she felt honour bound to explain to the compére that unfortunately she had not seen him on the telly, because we don't get Channel 5 in Cornwall, but he was doing a better job than he did last year, and she had thought that he was very good then.

After all the awards had finished, there was a magician, I took the liberty of in-

forming him that he did better tricks than the seals in a Zoo I know, and *they* pull in a large crowd. So if he needed a new location to perform his tricks, especially the catching of the ball on his nose one, then I could always put in a good word for him at the Zoo!

After all that was supposed to happen had finished, the pair of us sat talking with the winner of the "Best PhD student" rounding off the evening with a little extra drink or three, when these extremely attractive ladies came over to talk with Iwona and congratulate her on winning the award. In the middle of their talk with Iwona one turned to me and said: "Hi I'm Sam, I liked your report in Lab News are you going to do one for this year?"

I do not think Sam or her posse were too impressed as I sat there spluttering and choking over her name, as my brain raced through an alcoholic haze trying to work out how many more of `Mad Janet's` predictions were to come true. Fortunately Iwona's "ignore him he can't hold his wine" distracted them, and they resumed their congratulations to Iwona.

I didn't sleep much in the few hours that remained of the night when we got back to the hotel. We hadn't met `The Sponsor` or `The Watcher`, but what was worrying me more was why was the rooms fire alarm lights whizzing round when there was only one small LED in the unit? Then there was the conundrum of the room going round clockwise when in Cornwall the room span anti-clockwise when I was under the influence of alcohol?

The "Full English breakfast" had not sorted out my head as I sat with a stupid grin on my face in Paddington Station, attempting to people-watch. My first observation was that the people of London seemed to have given up on their "pretend pets" - you know those suitcases that they drag around because they can't have dogs - but more than likely they were moving so fast that my alcohol fogged eyesight just couldn't keep up with the action taking place in front of me.

Suddenly I saw someone I recognised. Now it is very difficult to be sure you have seen someone you know, especially if they are in a location other than their normal environment, but despite my alcohol induced haze I was pretty sure that I had seen my mate Tim - that would be Tim Smit of Eden Project fame. Now this was important because the Project had sponsored Iwona's application for the technician award. (A sponsor!)

I nudged Iwona and grunted and pointed in Tim's direction. By this time Tim was having his second look at Iwona and me because he was *just* as surprised to see someone he knew out of his or her natural environment. After what others could pass off as a family reunion on Platform 1, during which Tim and Iwona exchanged their usual continental kisses, (as apposed to those pretentious air

kisses that people give in big cities), and Tim and I exchanged manly handshakes, the news of Iwona's success was passed on. We headed in our separate directions, or rather he went off to 'Buck House' to receive the Albert Medal from Prince Philip, and we went back to our bench to wait for the train.

As I pointed out to Iwona; Tim can't put his award on the mantlepiece, but as *she* pointed out, it would be difficult for her to pin a kilo of glass to her chest! My eyebrow just twitched in an upward direction, but fortunately stopped just as Iwona threatened to slap me across the chops.

As I resumed my position on a bench grinning inanely, Iwona went off to check which platform the train was leaving from. Before going to check the train departure boards, she instructed me to nail Patrick Stewarts feet to the platform if I saw him.

When she returned I had a very stupid grin on my face, "You haven't puked have you?" she accused. I replied in the negative, and burst out laughing: "You never said anything about nailing Giles from Buffy to the station platform" (The Watcher! The final prophecy comes true!) Fortunately, there were some Station Police walking towards us, so that stopped me receiving what the rugby commentators describe as a "right good shoeing".

It is now some seventy-two hours after the awards, and as I look out at the village through my very dark sunglasses, I can see the remnants of the celebration party falling out of the pub. 'Mad Janet' had told everyone that Iwona was going to win, so they decided to hold a 'well-done' party for her even though she wasn't there. At exactly ten forty-five on the Tuesday evening, at the exact time Iwona's name as the winner was announced, Claire the barmaid declared the pub the site of a private party and the celebrations started.

Unfortunately Iwona could not party as much as she would have liked; the BBC and Carlton TV cameras were starting to roll as they each do a profile on her as the first Educational Technician to win an 'Industrial Technician of the Year' award. I wonder how she will cope behind her sunglasses; combine them with her sore throat from talking to the press all yesterday, it should be one heck of a performance. Why you may wonder is she getting so much media coverage?

Well, we do live in Cornwall and one of its residents winning such a prestigious award as the Laboratory News Best Technician of the Year Award is the biggest thing to happen down here since ..... Alex won "Fame Academy"

ARE WE SAD OR WOT?

For those of you with a computer that is connected to the Internet there is a really sad exercise you can carry out in the privacy of your own home. The result of which can produce hours of fun, but be warned it is a very dodgey exercise- type in your own name and press 'find'.

Fortunately it was not me who discovered this amusing distraction, but once you follow the lead of the comedian Dave Gorman - who was challenged to find 52 people called Dave Gorman utilising the Internet - it is surprising just what you get up to. Apparently earlier in the year, I played the drums in a rock band in front of tens of thousands of adoring fans in Brazil!

Sorry, as usual I digress. Chris burst into the office brandishing a piece of paper saying, "You have got to read this". The paper's contents were truly bizarre. In front of me was a computer translation of a radio report from Columbia that had been broadcast in Spanish - or was it Portuguese? - to the people of that nation. Believe it or not it looks as if Chris and I are "big" in Columbia, where apparently they avidly follow reports of the "Beast of Bodmin". This conjures up all sorts of fantasies, not least is the one about the drug barons in Columbia calling a halt to drug production while they listen with rapt attention to an update on the search for the "Beast". Perhaps the adventures of Chris and I are the Colombian equivalent of the "Archers"!

Caracol Colombia
www.caracol.com.co
▓▓To translate to the Ingles ▓▓

SUBJECT: SCIENCE
THE STRANGE CASE OF THE CORNUALLES BEAST

Source: EFÉ. Date: 7/23/98 8:00:00 A.m.

The " beast of Bodmin ", a strange animal that frightened the people who reside in hills of of this zone of the county of Cornualles (southwestern of England), can be an enormous wild cat, a species of European feline that was believed extinguished in the country from 1870.
For want of other subjects, given the summer time, the British press resorts every year to tell truculentas histories on trasgos, monsters and creepies-crawly, of which the cat at issue is not other peoplés
The investigation carried out the zoological one to it of the city of Newquay, in Cornualles, that mounted an operation that lasted five months and obtained a recording in video in which it appears the image of the feline.
After visionar the recording, an expert photographer, Pat Crowther, it declared that, in his opinion, the tape seems to last greater " but which is interrupted abruptly when the animal comes near to which it seems the bank of a park ", does difficult to calculate the size of the feline.
The experts of zoo calculate that the cat measures 50 centimeters of height by 108 of length, and has a tail of 32 to 40 centimeters. Also they have studied his tracks and excrements, and everything aims at that a wild cat unit of or European lynx is
The biologist and professor of Plymouth Chris Moiser, in the beginning, after observing the extracted photographies of the delvídeo animal, was escéptico, but it changed of opinion after examining the molds of the tracks. Moiser said then that " I am convinced that these claws do not belong to a cat, but to an animal of greater size, like a lynx ", and added " that the image that appears in the film not corresponds with this feline ", that pretends a much smaller bearing.
Between the people who assure to have observed " beast " appears the councilman of Cornualles Joan Vincent, whom it affirmed to have noticed the presence of one of those black felines near his house. " Era much greater than any cat than has never seen ", needed.
The proprietor of the zoological one of Newquay, Mike Thomas, said that " we are before a species nonidentified previously. Too small to be puma or a panther, but whose image in the video and the size of their tracks reveals that he is much more great that a domestic cat ".
For several years to this " beast " attacks to ewes robberies of babies in their cart and assaults to the solitary passers-by have been attributed to him who took a walk by the zone, reason why he has become a legend that remembers to the one of the monster of the Ness Lake, one of the greater celebrities of mitomanía British.
In a celebrated conference Tuesday and that it did not seem to convince to the hearing, Thomas it showed 20 seconds of the video caught by a farmer, of whom it is only known that John is called, in a not known place, and the stucco molds with the track of the animal.
Thomas has received critics that accuse of " opportunist " when doing public to him the findings of the video and the investigation made by their zoological one, which it could benefit from a massive affluence of public since now the children begin the vacations of summer.
Nevertheless, the democratic liberal deputy of the North of Cornualles Paul Tyler has showed that he will ask the Government who investigates the wild animal presence in the zone.
The British Ministry of Agriculture showed that it will have in consideration the tests, although in a 1995 report it reached the conclusion that there were no great felines in hills of Cornualles.
At the moment, the cat, if it exists, continues doing of hers and contributes to fill a hollow in some newspaper page. Cornualles is lost no an apex of its enormous tourist interest and, probably, until the next summer it does not

become to know nothing of this history, that, is or noncertain, at least " é trovata horseradish tree.

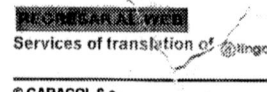
Services of translation of @lingo

© CARACOL S.a..

HAS THE CAT COME BACK?

The most puzzling aspect to this whole conundrum - apart from Lara the Lynx - is just what are people seeing, and if they are seeing something, where did it come from?

It is surprising how silly events trigger memories. In this case, I witnessed one of the largest men I have ever seen leading a very small dog on a lead, and almost instantaneously I was transported back to my childhood. For people of my generation the sight of Valerie Singleton of "Blue Peter" fame being dragged around by large "cats" was an annual event. In my minds eye, I pictured a struggling Val being dragged by an exceptionally large cat in a corner-shop, but where did she borrow it from?

After several excruciating minutes searching my memory files, a little light came on in the furthest recesses of my brain – Harrods. I recalled a quote from long ago that no matter what you wanted, if it was remotely possible, then Harrods was the place to go. You name it and they would get it!

I called Chris Moiser to discuss my hypothesis that the "Beast of Bodmin" could have come from Harrods, basing my theory on the you name it we will get it scenario. While Chris thought it was a possibility, he was more inclined to believe that the "Beast" could have been bought from an unscrupulous Zoo, as it would have been cheaper than going to Harrods.

The rationale behind Chris's argument was that while cubs are young and cute

they bring in the crowds. Unfortunately there comes a time when the cubs become economically unviable: i.e. they cost more to feed than the income they generate. For example: a lion eats somewhere in the region of six kg of meat a day, and a puma/leopard eats slightly less - approximately four to five kg a day. The average exotic cat produces somewhere in the region of four cubs at a time, so let us say that the cats breed once a year, and the Zoo starts with a pair of cats, by the end of two years they could possibly have a pride of ten. To house and feed ten exotic cats properly at the rate of five kg each every day takes a lot of money, even if the Zoo knows a friendly knackerman. So if someone offers you fifty quid for the cute cub in the corner....!

Despite looking for a conspiracy around every corner, I tend to believe that the vanity factor was a better option: i.e. "Look at my exotic cat, I got it from Harrods". It has that ring of class and decadence that the sort of person who would buy an exotic cat would need. The purchaser would, I believe see the ownership of an exotic cat as a status symbol and by purchasing it in Harrods all this criteria would be met, especially in Cornwall or Devon.

Filled with a belief that I was on to something new, I phoned Harrods. I explained my situation to a very nice lady on the switchboard, who listened patiently while I explained that I was after records of purchases of exotic cats. The records would probably have to be historical, because after the introduction of the 1976 Dangerous Wild Animals Act it was highly unlikely that Harrods would have sold any exotic cats.

The first port of call was the pet department, who were helpful in the extreme. They confirmed that they had not sold any large exotic animals for a very long time. However that did not stop customers phoning up with strange requests, and as hard as it is to believe in the twenty first century they had recently had enquiries regarding the purchase of a dolphin and an elephant! Unbelievable!

Apart from furnishing me with the information that man is still as stupid as ever, the pet department could not help me with my enquiries regarding exotic cats. However, they thought that the Archive Section might be able to assist me.

"Bingo". A nice lady from the Archive Section informed me that she remembered that she had seen some cuttings of celebrities and well known faces of the sixties and early seventies with exotic pets. While she could not swear that there were pictures of celebrities with exotic cats among the press cuttings, she would look into my request for information and foreword any relevant information to me.

True to their word, two days later a letter from Harrods crashed through the letterbox. Mr. Wormell - an Associate Archivist - had done a superb job. Not only

Harrods
KNIGHTSBRIDGE

Our ref: 235cr01q

2 May 2001

Dear Mr Crowther,

Thank you for your enquiry regarding exotic animals sold by Harrods in the 1960s and early 1970s.

Harrods Pet Department, also known as Harrods Zoo, sold a wide variety of animals in that period. In 1967 a baby elephant was sold to Leka, the son of King Zog of Albania, as a present for Governor Ronald Reagan of California. In 1968 a tapir called Veronica was on sale and bushbabies were also available. In 1969 two lion cubs were for sale in the department, costing £250 each (see the enclosed photocopy of an article from out house magazine *The Harrodian Gazette*). I believe that puma cubs were also sold in 1969, but I have no records of how many such animals were sold or to whom.

Needless to say, with today's far greater ecological awareness Harrods no longer sells such exotic animals.

We would be most interested in reading anything you write concerning the identity and origin of the "Beast of Bodmin".

Yours sincerely,

Sebastian Wormell
Associate Archivist

HARRODS LIMITED, KNIGHTSBRIDGE, LONDON SW1X 7XL TEL: 020 7730 1234 FAX: 020 7581 0470 www.harrods.com
REGISTERED IN LONDON 30209, REGISTERED OFFICE: 87-135 BROMPTON ROAD, KNIGHTSBRIDGE, LONDON SW1X 7XL

did he furbish me with information which allows me to inform you that Harrods Pet Department was also known as Harrods Zoo, but most importantly his letter and a photocopy of the *Harrodian Gazette* of December 1969 confirms that Harrods sold exotic cats.

The *Harrodian Gazette* has an article in it by Mr. R. Hazle (Buyer of Harrods Zoo) entitled "Pets at Christmas". In his article, Mr. Hazle outlines what an unusual present `Marcus` and `Marta` would make.

It transpires that Marcus and Marta were two-month-old tiger cubs that Harrods had acquired from a Devon Zoo. The cubs had taken over the "Zoo" at Harrods, but were beginning to settle down. Mr. Hazle goes on to point out that it will no doubt be a difficult task to find a home for them where they will be completely happy, but as in the case of the pumas he was confident that it would work out well in the end.

In case you are interested Marcus and Merta were on sale for £250 each, and that is in 1969! I am please to report that Mr. Hazle went on to write that in his opinion it was probably better for the average customer to buy a gerbil for their children's Christmas present, as not only did the gerbils only cost fifteen shillings (or seventy five pence in current currency), Mr. Hazle assured readers that the gerbils might be a little less inclined to cause the chaos that could be caused by including Marcus or Marta among the presents under the Christmas tree.

So now I have found at least one legitimate supplier of exotic cats, and Chris assures me that there are other legitimate suppliers. Which could be traced relatively easily through *Cage and Aviary Bird* from the early sixties through to the seventies.

There now exists the possibility that exotic cats exported from Devon Zoos returned to the counties of Devon and Cornwall only to be released on to the Moors when the 1976 Dangerous Wild Animals act was introduced. Harrods reports confirm that they sold lions and pumas, therefore it is probably safe to say that between Harrods and the other legitimate suppliers of exotic cats, the "Beast of Bodmin" could well have at some stage in its life been someone's pet.

CAN YOU LOOK AT OUR VIDEO?

In late September (way past the press silly season) the Local *Sunday Independent* ran a story accompanying a photograph extracted from a video film which the paper claimed was of the "Beasts" of Bigbury, not one "Beast" but two! By chance the reporter recorded that the footage was to be viewed by "experts" but the article did not say who the experts were to be. Never one to miss a chance to get my name in print I was on the phone to them in a flash, and low and behold Chris and I became said experts. Below is the article/report that was submitted to the *Sunday Independent*.

What happens when an "expert" looks at a Video of the "Beast"?

If you want to become a Big Cat expert without having to go through all the hassle of a zoological education, there are two resources you might consider using. The first is the seminal 11 volumes of work entitled *Animal Locomotion*. These are the 100,000 photographic studies of animal movements by Eadweard Muybridge. Unfortunately the cost of these books is extremely prohibitive when it comes to buying them. If you are lucky the library might let you have a look at the books, if they have a copy. If they do have a copy of the books you can rest assured that they will be behind a locked cabinet, and you will be one of the very few people to ask to see them.

The second option and the one that I favour - are the films of Walt Disney. Yes that's right, the films of Walt Disney - let me explain. When Walt started to produce his cartoons, the artists drawing the characters spent hours and hours studying the movement of the animals that they converted into the characters that we love so much. The movement of the animals in these films is as near perfect as it is possible to create. So as I am a "Beast" expert my favourite films are *"The Jungle Book"* and *"Aristocats"*. The logic behind this selection is obvious, in the *Jungle Book* there is the excellent 'Bagheera' the Panther, and in the *Aristocats* there are so many cat varieties to watch, that it is a veritable gold mine of feline movement.

Armed with this highly specialised visual input, it was with great excitement that I awaited the arrival of the video of the "Beast" that a local newspaper was supplying for inspection. The team of experts was assembled (Chris Moiser, Biology Lecturer, and myself), the College's Media Department's video-editing suite was booked, the seating suitably arranged so that the paper's photographer could capture the astonished looks on the experts faces as they viewed actual footage of the "Beast".

As it was, it was fortunate that the photographer didn't come to photograph the great event. The lights were dimmed as the equipment sprang into life, the screen flickered, and the sighs of disappointment were exhaled, as once again as we found ourselves looking at a video of - yes you guessed it - "domestic moggies". How did my co-expert and I know we were looking at domestic or at best farm cats?

I am afraid the evidence was plain to see. Firstly there were two of them, a rarity in the wild. Most big cats are solitary, except during the mating season. Secondly, the short thistles in the field were higher than the cats. Thirdly one of the cats jumps out of its skin while it walks down the hill; a "Beast" would have attacked what ever had disturbed it. (Who am I to write - think John Prescott) While I must admit a large degree of disappointment; it was nothing compared to the near anger that my co-watcher was expressing.

At this point, I feel it is important to explain that the "experts" or at least those I associate with, are believers. Between us we have seen enough evidence to probably prove that there are exotic cats roaming Devon, Cornwall and other areas in the UK. What we have not seen "yet" is the photographic proof that will convince the rest of the world that these animals exist. If you believe that you have such a picture or video footage please watch Disney's' *"The Jungle Book"* before you offer your images up for examination by the general public, and by association the experts. At worse you will have watched an enjoyable video together with all those catchy tunes to sing along with. At best, if your footage or picture looks a dead ringer for Bagheera then you will make history and a small fortune for yourself.

So how did the article appear in the paper the following Sunday ?
"Beast" expert says watch Disney Videos!

When things get a little slow on the "Beast" front I find myself being asked to examine the contents of photographs and videos of what are purported to be mysterious and exotic creatures. The following is a report I submitted to *Animals & Men* in July 2002.

LITTLE PRICKS AND A SHAG OR – AUGUST COMES EARLY IN 2002 FOR THE CORNISH GUARDIAN.

For those of you who don't live in Cornwall, I have important news for you. While the rest of you have been going "Bananas" over the Golden Jubilee, the English Football team and dare I write it ("Go on Paul, write it" I hear you say) Tim "Bloody" Henman. The people of Cornwall have been smouldering away in the toe end of England. Firstly, Johnny "Two Jabs" Prescott mumbled something about regional councils, then said that Cornwall could not have one – the result, an instant petition of complaint signed by nearly the whole population of Cornwall or rather those that still talk in Cornish. Then there was the thorny issue of that great tourist attraction, the "Beast of Bodmin". Not much news on that front, but that's OK because the tourist figures are on the up. What the tourist industry needs is a boost from another direction. Something, which that illegitimate Crowther could not screw up for them.

So what did they come up with this time? Morgawr or as the *Western Morning News* put it – *"The West Country Nessie"* (Blimey, I can hear the sound of flapping plastic bags on car roof racks thundering down the A30 as I write!)

Just my luck - unbeknown to me - I had been volunteered by Mike Thomas of Newquay Zoo, as an expert to examine the video footage and give an opinion to the *Cornish Guardian* on the video's contents. So, to cut a very long story short, I found myself in this fellow's spare bedroom looking at videos! (It's OK, the room was the man's video lab, and wow what a lab. It was just like being in the *Man who fell to Earth*) Once I had found a TV screen that I could focus on, I sat back and got myself into a suitable 'cosmic' state.

First I watched the footage at normal speed. Very interesting! In the video, the operator clearly states that he thinks he was filming a "Killer Whale". I wonder how does the man go from Killer Whale to Morgawr in three years? (The footage was shot in the summer of '99) Then I watched it one frame at a time. Next, I was asked to give my opinion on the footage as I watched it again one frame at a time. In the three minutes of footage (including footage of the cameraman's wife floating in the sea (she was alive and not the subject of the enquiry, I hasten to add), I managed to change my opinion four times. In chronological order my guesses were: 1) A wooden sleeper used for ballast in a ship. 2) A sea bird, a shag (Hence second part of the title). 3) A seal, and fourth, and most importantly of all – not a F***ing clue. I left my newly acquired video friend in agreement that probably someone will look at the stills from the video which were to be published in the following evening's *Cornish Guardian* and say "That's a ...."

That night I didn't sleep that well. It felt as if someone was pricking me in various intimate parts of my body, (see the first part of the title). Fortunately my wife assured me it was not her trying to wake me up to do the squishy thing with her. Voodoo I thought! This is a sign that I'm going to crack this little problem. (You can tell, I am very sensitive to cosmic vibes).

Sure enough the following day, I met a Zoology graduate from Birmingham University in a pet shop, (as you do). The man took one look at the pictures in the paper and said:"That's a Sun fish"! There then followed a series of phone calls to the MBA at Plymouth, and other marine specialists who all thought my effort at subject identification was about 95% correct.

There then followed an extremely short interview with a DJ called Laurence on *Radio Cornwall*. I must confess that he was not too impressed with my analysis of the video's content. Come to think of it neither was the wife of the man who had shot the video, she hung up when I told her the results of my investigation. However the cameraman called a few days later, and I think it is fair to say we parted amicably, and agreed to differ on the videos' content.

I can live with a 95% probability of the video's contents being a Sun Fish, be-

cause just a few weeks ago two new species of monkey were discovered on land and who else lives on land – yep you have guessed it – Man. Now man doesn't live in the sea, yet! So the number of unidentified species living in the oceans is incalculable, so this leaves a 5% possibility that the video could be of, as the *Western Morning News* put it – The Cornish Nessie! But, sorry, not this time, good effort, but just like the "Beast of Bodmin" – keep the footage and pictures coming in, some day we will see the real thing and I don't mean a bottle of Coke!

Post revelation events

Imagine, I spent all that effort trying to identify the contents of this bod's video, and what happens? There is no report of my efforts in any of the newspapers. Hell, even Mike Thomas, who had nothing what so ever to do with the search for the identity of the sea monster, was quoted in the *Western Morning News* offering my information as the answer. Richard of the CFZ appeared on Carlton Westcountry television twenty-four hours after the footage was shown on the local new spot. What did he say? It's a bloody bird! There just aint no justice. (Anyone would think I am envious …. Too bloody true I was.)

It would appear that as soon as one story on the mysterious is printed in the daily newspapers in the SW there develops an instantaneous rash of them. The *Sunday Independent* led the way this time. One week after the sea serpent story broke, there was a report on the Mike Thomas "Beast" story from five years earlier. The *Western Morning News* followed that up with a story concerning a woman who saw a large cat with a rabbit in its' mouth. The woman said that the cat was mottled brown and had pointy ears. At this stage like me you are probably thinking Lynx! Alas, she then describes it as having a fluffy tail, and having a body length of three foot!

Once again the press have hyped up a story. Why don't they try reverse psychology? Next time perhaps if they wrote a headline saying - *Woman sees cat with a rabbit in its mouth* things may progress to the stage where people may even report *proper* sightings of the "Beasts"!

THE BEAST AND I

IS THIS THE LAST OF MIKE THOMAS?

August 2003 proved to be vaguely interesting in the search for the elusive "Beast", but I think it has something to do with Mike Thomas retiring from Newquay Zoo.

I knew that Mike was going to retire sooner rather than later, so there was no shock in that, but what was slightly bizarre was the sudden flurry of "Beast" activity reported in the *Cornish Guardian* with Mike's smiling face above the reports. The first sighting was based around an image taken by a man from Manchester - in Cornwall on holiday - and the claims that it was the "Beast" were backed up by other experts who had done photoanalysis of the image, and had confirmed the image was genuine.

I phoned Mike up that evening to find out more about the image, and his experts. Imagine my surprise when he said, "It's you, dear boy". I was flabbergasted, so flabber was my gasted that I had to sit down and have a large Scotch when I put the phone down. I must have looked bad, because even Iwona showed concern. As I sat trying to reconnect long defunct neural pathways bit-by-bit it came back to me.

In February or some time earlier in the year, Mike had sent me an image of something apparently running across a field. I say apparently because the image was of the usual high class - blurred and out of focus. I scanned it into the computer and played around with it, and printed off the results for Chris Moiser and me to look at. The outcome - as I recall - was undeterminable, but very probably not the "Beast".

I reported back to Mike the results of Chris's and my evaluation, and he appeared to except it. We decided that we needed more evidence. Mike was optimistic because our Manchester snapper was part of a group who had seen it, and Mike hoped that others in the group might have better pictures. Mike had the man's address, and would write to him. Over the summer I called into the zoo for a coffee and a chat. During one of our chats, Mike told me that unfortunately none of the others in the man from Manchester's group had taken a photograph of the "Beast" As far as I was concerned that was it, case closed – insufficient evidence.

Then two weeks later there was dramatic news on all the local television news bulletins. *"Definitive Beast footage"*. This was it; the video recorder was set up and I waited on the edge of my seat. Three minutes later I was kicking up great clouds of wood chip, sucking on my pipe furiously. He had done it again! This time it was worse you could see the collar on the bloody moggy!

Before I reached my smoking seat at the back of the garden, the phone started ringing. Iwona came to the door and yelled, "You get that, I'm not dealing with your nutty "Beast" friends and the press". Sure enough, it *was* the press, and my nutty friends all wanting quotes and comments. I phoned Mike up during a lull in the ringing.

Apparently, in his estimation, the collar was a shadow. That was his story and he was sticking to it despite my pointing out that the shadow did not move as the cat ran.

I reported back to my friends in the press that there was a conflict in what was being seen, mainly the collar, but that it was my belief that it was a domestic cat despite eyewitness reports and the footage.

What can I say about my mate Mike?

He is a good man. He has raised Newquay Zoo from 60,000 visitors a year when he took it over, to 250,000 now that he has sold it as a very much going concern. Newquay Zoo is a great place to go and spend the best part of a day wandering around, the animals are thriving, and breeding like animals should do; it is a very nice medium sized zoo. How much of the zoo's success is down to the

"Beast". I will let you decide, but there is a good display of paw prints to look at. I'll miss my chats with Mike.

Just to prove that it's a small world, the man the new owners of the Zoo have installed as the new manager - the man from Sheldon where all this started, isn't life funny.

THE USUAL SUSPECTS

By a process of extrapolation, the following list of exotic cats are the species that I feel are the "best fit" for the "Beast of Bodmin Moor". By cross referencing exotic cat biological information and eyewitness accounts, the following are possible "best case fits". The list is by no means definitive. There are people who believe that the "Beast" could be a hybrid, a cross between domestic cats and some form of wildcat. There are those who believe it could be an American bobcat - the list of possibilities could be endless, and certainly makes for lively after-dinner conversation, but as I have said, based on the biological evidence and the press reports, the following are my choice.

PUMA *(Felis concolor)*

The Puma is the prime suspect, as its biological description does tend to fit the eyewitness descriptions of the "Beast".

Length Of Head and Body   100cm – 190cm
Length of tail   55cm – 80cm
Weight   40 – 100Kg

These are for both male and female, the smallest and lightest end of the scale corresponds to the female.

Colouring: The Puma has a plain coat with no patterning on it, the colour tends to vary between sandy grey, and a fox like red depending on the Puma's environment. Puma's undersides and bellies tend to be white (if clean).

There are reports of melanistic pumas, i.e. pumas which are black, being reported in South America. While black pumas are a rarity, this strengthens the possibility of a melanistic puma being the "Beast". The owner of such a cat would see themselves has having a good deal of kudos in the circles of people who had this type of creature as a pet. However when things got out of control because the cat got too big or cost too much to feed, they would release it into the wild because as they would no doubt have put it: "It is the best thing for the cat".

Environment: The puma can survive in a wide variety of habitats. In its natural environment, it is found in regions as diverse as tropical rain forests to grassland and scrub. All the puma needs is some form of shelter, a water supply

and a food source.

Given these requirements, Bodmin Moor is an ideal habitat. There is a good water supply, there is cover in the form of small woods, and most importantly there is a good food supply. Not only is there a good supply of rabbits, voles and other small mammals, but also - when the conditions are against them - man supplies the odd meal in the form of livestock.

Pumas can swim, run and jump. In the case of jumping, there are reports of pumas leaping up to ten foot into trees to catch prey. When pumas are chased in their natural habitat, they tend to jump into trees and stay there until nightfall. pumas tend to be nocturnal, hunting at dusk and travelling throughout their territory at night. Puma's territory tend to be approximately twenty five miles in radius, they tend to hunt in one site for two days to a maximum of three days in any one site, this leads one to conclude that pumas are very good at "farming" their prey.

LYNX *(Felis lynx)*

Length of Head and Body 80cm – 130cm
Length of tail   60cm - 75cm
Weight   18 - 35Kg

The lynx is not far off the dimensions of a large domestic cat with slightly longer hair on its coat. While there have been sightings of excessively large domestic cats being mistaken for the "Beast", the lynx is a very efficient hunter and so sightings would be very unusual, and there have been no reports that mention the Lynx's distinctive fluffy tipped ears.

Colouring: The Lynx tends to be a grey colour, however they can be yellow/brown. In certain areas like Central and Southern Europe they can be found with black spots on their flanks.

Environment: The Lynx tends to prefer an environment where there is dense forestation and undergrowth. In parts of the Himalayas, the lynx does live in rocky outcrop regions. However there are dense scrub boltholes close at hand.

The lynx is a solitary hunter, and hunts mainly at dawn and dusk. They tend to spend most of their time sleeping. The lynx has the most phenomenal eyesight; it is reputed to be able to see a mouse at 75 meters and a roe deer at 600m.

The range and size of prey that a lynx takes is staggering when you take into

account its size. Lynx will take anything from hares to wild boar. In certain parts of Sweden, lynx have even been seen taking reindeer.

The lynx tends to have a relatively small territory some times as small as 1,000 hectares however they have been known to travel in excess of 450 kilometres in a ten-week period when their food source dries up.

LEOPARD *(Panthera pardus)*

Length of Head and Body 95cm. – 1.70 metres
Length of tail   45cm. - 1.00 metre
Weight   35 – 55 Kg

The leopard is a big cat. However its normal colouring precludes it from being the "Beast".

Colouring: The traditional leopard has black melanistic spots on a straw coloured background, the throat and belly tend to be white. There are totally melanistic leopards. Up close black leopards - or black panthers, as they are also known - are not a smooth, consistent, black. Their colouring is a form of optical illusion; their black coat is made up of tightly packed black rosettes, so the normal straw coloured background is swamped out.

Environment: The leopard has a wide variety of habitats. There are even reports of leopards being seen in the vicinity of the snowline, from this it is possible to conclude that leopards can exist in snow, however because of the limitation of food in the perma-snow regions, I believe that the leopard can survive perfectly adequately where the snow covers the land for a short period in the year. Leopards are nomadic by nature and can travel between twenty-five and seventy-five kilometres a night.

It is hard to give an accurate assessment of a leopard's hunting profile. The majority of studies have been in African National Parks, where there is a concentration of "Hunters", therefore their activities may have become modified to suit their environment. In the parks, leopards have been seen hunting during daylight hours. Studies outside the parks would tend to describe the leopard as a nocturnal animal.

The leopard tends to stalk its prey until it is close enough for a quick strike. The strike has been recorded as having a speed in excess of 60 kilometres per hour. Once a kill has taken place, and the leopard fed to its fill, the cat then stores the prey up a tree to keep it away from scavengers. Leopard kills have been found as high as three and a half metres up trees. There was one report of the "Beast" having hauled its prey up a tree in Devon. The circumstances were a little peculiar at the time and despite confirmation of the kill, and an assurance from a vet that the cause was a leopard attack, there have been no further reports in the ensuing years so based on the lack of further evidence I feel inclined to discount the leopard as the "Beast".

JAGUAR (Panthera onca)

Length of Head and Body 1 metre - 2 meters
Length of Tail   40 cm.- 70cm
Weight   36 Kg - 158 Kg

The jaguar is a very large, heavily built cat.

Colouring: The average jaguar has a background colour of pale yellow to a rusty red. The background is covered by black rosettes which cover the back and flanks. The tail has black hoops on it and the belly and inside legs are white. It has been noted that cats from open ground are slightly lighter than those from heavily forested regions, this would be logical in terms of camouflage in the said areas.

There have been recorded sightings of total melanistic jaguars. In some areas black jaguars out number "normal jaguars".

Environment: Jaguars have a diverse habitat and appear to live in all areas except desert and permasnow. Studies show that the jaguar is nocturnal in its hunting habits. Jaguars have been seen swimming across rivers while they are on hunting expeditions.

The jaguar tends to eat mammals, and when it has had its fill it retreats to a hiding place to digest the food, before returning for a further feed at a later time. Jaguars have been known to take horses this lead to speculation of the "Beast" being a jaguar when there were reports of damage to horses in Devon and Cornwall. However, there were other explanations for the reported horse mutilations.

The jaguar has been known to drag its prey over considerable distances before they eat their prey. To date there have been no reports of bloody tracks leading to the sight of a carcass.

1000000001000001
ANALYSE THAT!

When I was a photographic lecturer, I took great delight in showing students examples of "cooked" images, or to use the "in" words of 2003, "sexed-up" images.

Recently there have been two images of note that have brought the integrity of photography in question. Both images were taken as part of the war coverage in Iraq, and both photographers were duly relieved of their post. You will note that I referred to them as photographers, not technicians. Why? They used digital cameras.

As the photographic consultant for the CFZ I get the job of analysing images - predominantly - of the "Beast" of Bodmin. This is not as hard a job you may think. The longest I have spent checking out the authenticity of an image is a month, and it was solved once we saw the negatives of the "Beast" sat beside a couple of bricks. But it is going to get harder – a lot harder.

Digital photography is booming. You can hardly fail to notice the number of digital cameras that are appearing at weddings these days, but what about image storage? If pushed, you could probably find the negatives of that wedding you went to five years ago, they are in a drawer or some box or other, but what if

they were digital?

With a digital camera, your first action would have been to cull the images down to those you wanted. To do that you just press `delete`. Then you might have stored them on your hard-drive while you were selecting the ones you were printing. Then, oops there they go! Deleted, when you needed more hard drive space. Still, it doesn't matter. I remember the event - I don't need the pictures to remind me what happened. Then the bride phones you up to ask you for a copy of a picture. "Sorry luv I've deleted them." Suppose you are diligent and you have saved them onto a disk - let's say a floppy, but ten years later. What are floppy disks? Remember the laser disk! Storage is going to be a major problem when it comes to archiving historical images taken with digital equipment.

So where am I going, and what has all this to do with Cryptozoology? I am currently - as they say - `between jobs`, and I need money (approximately £60,000 to get rid if the mortgage.) In my dreams I have a digital SLR camera. I have the know how and the equipment to produce the ultimate fake image. If I wanted to fool the world then here is how I would do it:

How to earn a shed load!

1) Take one hardboard cut-out of a puma/leopard
2) Place it in shrubs in a location of natural beauty.
3) Make sure that there are no tell-tale signs of human involvement, no foot prints leading to the cut-out etc.
4) Take a series of images of the "Beast".
5) Go home and examine the images in great detail on the computer just to check it out for visual faults.
6) Delete all the other images on the camera's storage system. Most digital cameras can keep picture six in the same place when the others are deleted all around it.
7) Go out and use up pictures 1-5 and 7- X and rush to the nearest newspaper office.

Why will this work? Why will the likes of me not be able to challenge the image? Simple. It boils down to the photographer's word against mine, and no solicitor should allow you get involved in a war of words. After all, all the photographer was doing was going out to photograph a site of natural beauty, how can I or anyone else question his or her motive? It is not their fault that I do not believe their story and their image.

A well-prepared trickster would have all the answers. Why aren't there any other pictures of the "Beast"? The batteries ran out! And the "Beast" had gone

by the time I changed them! It was the last frame on the system (this works for film, but remember the previous 25/23 frames - I will want to see them!) What will I, the debunker, have to use? One frame off a digital storage system. This is as much use to me as a one-legged man in an arse-kicking contest. The photographer wins, goes past go, and collects the payment for their mortgage. All they have to hope for is that someone didn't see them, or know that they have read this book. No one "dobs" on tricksters quicker than those who are jealous! Especially when money is involved.

CATASTROPHE

This is two stories in one; the first is an abomination, the second is simply a catastrophe. It all starts with a cat that weighs up to 35 pounds, though some breeders claim to have variations of the breed weighing up to and beyond 100 pounds. It must be noted that these extraordinary heavyweight cats are regarded as a bit of a myth, even on the cats many web sites. Said cats have an excessively long body, that makes them look like their feline ancestors, which prior to the 1970s is what they were. So what will one of these things set you back? The answer is in excess of £400, and the nearer your cat is in marking to its original wildcat ancestors, so the price rockets to closer to £1,000. By now you are thinking that if I had one of these things I'd lock it up in a gilded cage. Well in some circles that is the case. Except in Lancashire where if they see them they shoot them on sight, and get them stuffed. (More later). This costly moggy has crashed into the feline top ten at number eight, they have featured in a Nationwide advertising campaign for a chain of women's accessories, and if you are to believe the veterinary assistances in St. Austell, (and I do), there are over one hundred of these things in mid-Cornwall alone.

In the mis-plagiarised words of Rolf Harris - have you guessed what I am wittering on about yet? Given all the clues, the answer can only be one thing: The very expensive, but not so rare in mid –Cornwall, `Bengal Cat`!

So how the heck did the CFZ photographic analyst get involved with expensive moggies ? As usual it all follows on from a telephone call. (Catastrophe One coming up). There I was sat one Sunday evening just before Christmas, once again fretting over Gollie and Mollies relationship, in that Sunday evening bubblegum for the brain that is *"Monarch of the Glen"* when the phone rang. I don't feel this is the place to tell you who was phoning, but their voice was verging on the incredulous when they told me that a farmer in Lancashire had shot a bengal cat for apparently worrying his chickens. If that was not bad enough he had shot the wrong one. The bengal he thought he had shot turned up

a few hours later to continue its' predations. Still, undeterred, the farmer was in the process of having the cat he shot stuffed, so that he could claim that he had shot the "Beast" of "somewhere" in Lancashire.

As the owner of two cats - one of whom (Tiger) terrorises the neighbourhood with alacrity and is instantaneously at the side of anyone opening the bonnet of a car because he thinks he is the reincarnation of Isombard Kingdom Brunel or perhaps it is Colin Chapman - I was somewhat taken aback by what I had heard. After distressing my wife with the story, we just sat there looking at our cats wondering what we would have done if the shithead that had shot Tiger had succeeded in assassinating him.

Suddenly the boss leaped to her feet, and yelled: "I've got it, let's scare the heck out of the farmer by telling him that the cat was probably chipped, if we had a cat which was that expensive we would have it chipped"! If the taxidermist found a chip he would have to report it to the police, RSPCA,.... ! I think it is fair to assume that in the location of the incident there are no `back street taxidermists!` Even if there was, the minute the farmer showed his prize exhibit to the public, someone would identify it for what it was, and as they say: "The cat would be out of the bag". So the seeds of revenge were sown to my friend for him to pass back down the phone lines of Britain.

It is surprising how fast things move when people think that they are up to their neck in it! In less than an hour the phone rang again; it was my friend once again to tell me that we had caused absolute pandemonium, and the farmer had been on the phone to the taxidermist to check whether the cat had been chipped. Unfortunately it had not, but at least the farmer would have second thoughts before he blasted away with his shotgun the next time. I just hope his little venture cost him a very large dry cleaning bill!

All this led me to wonder about the population of Bengal Cats in Mid Cornwall. (Catastrophe Two coming up, and this is potentially a big un!) I initiated my search by casually asking my vet how many "Bengal's" were on their books, and was astonished by the reply of twenty-seven.

This was then followed by a visit to a vet centre near St. Austell Station. After a brief introduction and explanation of my quest, the vet's receptionist responded by saying: "we have loads of them on our books". She continued: "We neutered one of them yesterday". My spluttering of: "are people that rich in Cornwall that they can have what to me would have been a £400 plus investment knackered, I'd have the thing making luvvv twenty four hours a day, seven days a week to recoup my money". was followed by her saying "Bengal Cats are more common than Siamese cats down here"!

Several phone calls later, the number of bengal cats within a ten-mile radius of St. Austell was in excess of one hundred. This must make mid-Cornwall the most densely populated area of bengal cats in the UK. There was further news - one was missing!

I dived into my archives and discovered that a high percentage of the "Beast" sightings were of a Brown/Golden Brown coloured cat, and the word leopard also cropped up fairly regularly. Could these sighting have been bengals?

In my excitement, I phoned my press contacts to warn them of an imminent sighting of the "Beast", and warned them as to what it might be. The strangest call I made was to the *Plymouth Evening Herald* offices. I didn't get my contact, but it appears that the staff were following up on a story they were doing on bengal cats, and independently, they had come up with a similar conclusion. I don't know if the journalists have the time or inclination, but there were murmurs of agreement when I suggested that the showing pictures of bengal cats to the readers who claim to have seen the "Brown Beast", might produce interesting responses.

If my prediction does come true where does leave me/us? Have I given the cryptozoologists and "Beast" spotters food for thought, as opposed to food for the stomach at this festive time? Or, given that a leading "Beast" expert who I have worked with responded to my theory by saying "keep it quiet, as it would be nice to maintain the mystery", have I have leapt in where only fools tread?

As much as I would like to think that I have gone some way to clearing up the mystery of the "Beast of Bodmin", in my heart I hope I haven't. It would be a catastrophe if I weren't sat at my computer still analysing images of the "Beast" and upsetting the general public by rubbishing their images of "Beasts" for decades to come. Then again I really would like to be the one to confirm an image as being the definitive photograph of the "Beast of Bodmin".

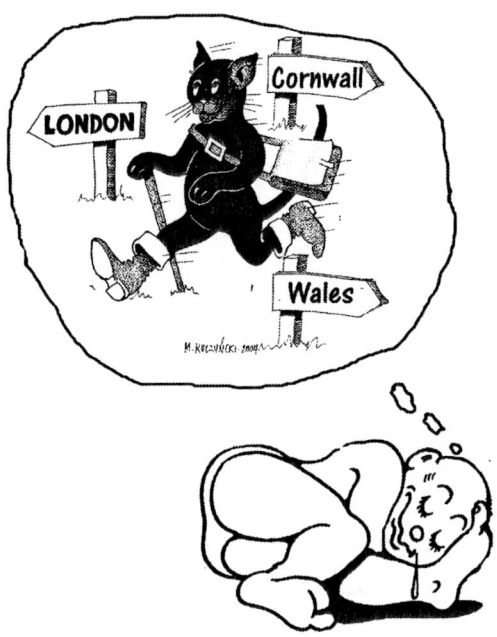

IT IS NOT JUST THE CORNISH, YOU KNOW! EVERYONE WANTS ONE!

There are days when you just can't believe what you are hearing. I was lying in bed the other evening, no, sorry, I was, as I had told my wife, listening to a football match on "*Five Live*", in no way shape or form was I catching 40 Z's.

The checking my eyelids for light leakage was interrupted by a newsreader informing me that a large black cat had attacked a man in London. The story continued... The man had called the police and an ambulance, and a police officer had seen the attacker out of the corner of his eye, and an armed response team had been called in, and an area had been sealed off with the residents being advised to stay indoors.

You have to admit this is a story ripe for investigation, especially after Lara. Maybe London *is* crawling with large exotic cats just waiting an opportunity to

devour the human population. There was nothing else to do but turn on the computer and start going through the internet to try and find out what had happened. There it was - care of the BBC news sites - all you ever needed to know about the attack.

From the radio report it would appear that our cockney feline version of `Crocodile Dundee` went out into his back garden to rescue his distressed mog who was involved in a little feline altercation. Sticking his head where only the brave would, (i.e. into a bush where the sound of two mogs having a singing contest was being held), he fell over, as one of the contestants shot out of said bush at approximately head height, and started having a wrestling match with the singing contest interloper.

In his distressed state, the man duly called the police and ambulance. The former started a search for this monstrous cat, and the latter tended the interloper's wounds. The police, being - well one can only describe them as - the police, instantaneously sealed off an area around the scene of the incident, and called for armed backup. Meanwhile the ambulance paramedics treated our hero for minor scratches, and a bit of bruising following his tumble, which resulted from his bending down and the cat shooting out of the bush. In other words the shock of the cat coming out of the bush caused him to tumble over! This you must agree must have been a situation which called for a new pair of brown trousers for our intrepid hero!

So, m'Lord, at this point I feel I must draw your attention to the reports over the first three days after the incident on the Internet. On the Internet the incident was reported c/o BBC News/London as having happened as follows: basically the same as above until you get to the point of the cat coming out of the bush. Here the story differs from the above. At BBC/News/London it said that the man, (height six foot and weighing in at approximately fifteen stones) almost had a `best of three falls` wrestling match, with a cat the size of a Labrador dog. At this point I feel justified in reminding you of the man's injuries – slight scratches and bruising from his tumble!

Wow! A cat the size of a Labrador! This requires further investigation, so where better to start a new search than the *Cbeebies* web site, and, yes, here was another report on the incident. As before, the report followed what I have already reported, but …... and here it gets *even* better! This time, our hero was attacked by a "Big Black Cat over six foot in length" which had gone for him. Remember his injuries and think `six-foot big black cat`! Even with my imagination, I couldn't make it up like these people do.

Why do they do it? Well due to possible legal implications I leave the question as a rhetorical one, but this led me to investigate other sightings because things

have gone very quiet down here in Cornwall, but judging from reports from the rest of the UK. "Beasts" are springing up all over the place and thanks to the *South London Guardian* web site I found loads of sighting in London to investigate. Well, when I write `investigate`, I mean `peruse and ignore`.

The London sites have several pictures, which I have to confess left me speechless, or more accurately I was silent because I was in agony from having crossed my legs a little too high up, and a little too quickly, in an effort to stop me peeing my pants. With the exception of the photos of Lara, they were badly taken pictures of dogs and domestic cats backed up with stories of further sightings in Cumbria, Devon or Cornwall.

If the articles weren't illustrated by badly-taken photographs of domestic cats and dogs, the articles themselves were so naïve that the degree of investigation by the writers is bordering on the non-existant. One article went as far as to write that the majority of sightings were between 6 and 10 pm, 6 – 10 at night, need I write more. Is it any wonder that recently *Fortean Times* said that an excessively high number of sightings were false, and even went as far as questioning the existence of exotic cats roaming the British countryside.

Despite the *Fortean Times* getting bored with big cat stories, and local British press writing sloppy reports of sightings of them, it would appear that the rest of the world just can't get enough of them.

Word has been smuggled out from the house of the man involved in the `wrestling match` with the cat that morphs from the size of a Labrador to a feline monster with a length in excess of six foot. Apparently the man has been bitten down to the bone of his hand (according to the Paramedics who wanted to take him to hospital (Big cat biting down to the bone!) This said, the big news is that the man is scared to leave his house for two reasons:

1) He is scared of the cat getting him again (true). I am sorry, but the idea of a cat - big or otherwise - baring a grudge against this fellow, is perhaps a little too far-fetched. Maybe the man has watched *Jaws* too many times for his own good, or perhaps he used to be a postman who was used to being attacked by little snappy dogs as he posted letters? Who knows?

2) His house is under siege from the world's press (true). Now, based on my experience preceding and following the "Beast" debate, I could have told him that this is what would happen. Heck, I ended up as a racing tipster on a New Zealand radio station, because they had to go to the 6 o'clock race at Christchurch during my interview. What did *not* happen to me was "allegedly" an all expenses paid trip for the family to

appear on American television. Now I don't know if he got over his agoraphobia to take up this offer, but I bet you would and I *definitely* would.

I got involved in the big cat debate as a result of my trying to establish whether or not these cats existed. I use my scientific abilities and my photographic experiences to question photographs of exotic cats published in newspapers in the westcountry. In this time I have been called ` Mr. Pompous` or ` Mr. Arrogant`, I have been threatened with legal action by the people who have received large sums of money for charities of their choice or their own financial gain, yet I have continued with my investigations, in the hope that one day I will see the definitive image of the "Beast" of wherever.

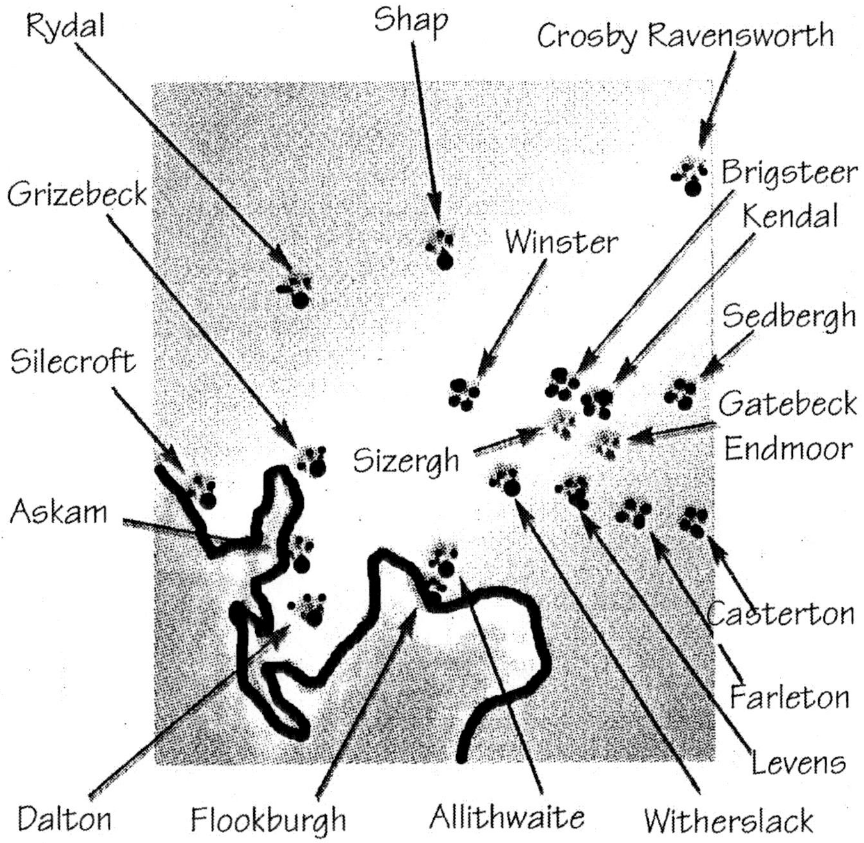

OOP NORTH

This is a map of the South lakes and Furness area of North West England. As you can see there are a large number of sightings in a relatively small area over a short period of time and still no one can produce an image of the Beast! That said given the terrain and the potential food supply to feed a large cat this area is just as good as any for a big cat to survive in the wilds of Britain than any other. But you have to wonder why is this map and the press reports associated with it to be found when looking through London Local Papers. Is the distribution of sightings leading to more sightings because people who are susceptible to seeing Big Cats, UFO's etc are reading about other peoples sightings and trying to "get on the band wagon"?

DATE LINE - 16th April 2005

Sun Newspaper published a picture of a toy Panther

The photograph was verified as:

" *Really important photo. It proves there are big cats wild in Britain*"

                         Founder of the British Big Cat Society

The following is a near real time report on the actions taken by myself and Chris Moiser following this publication.

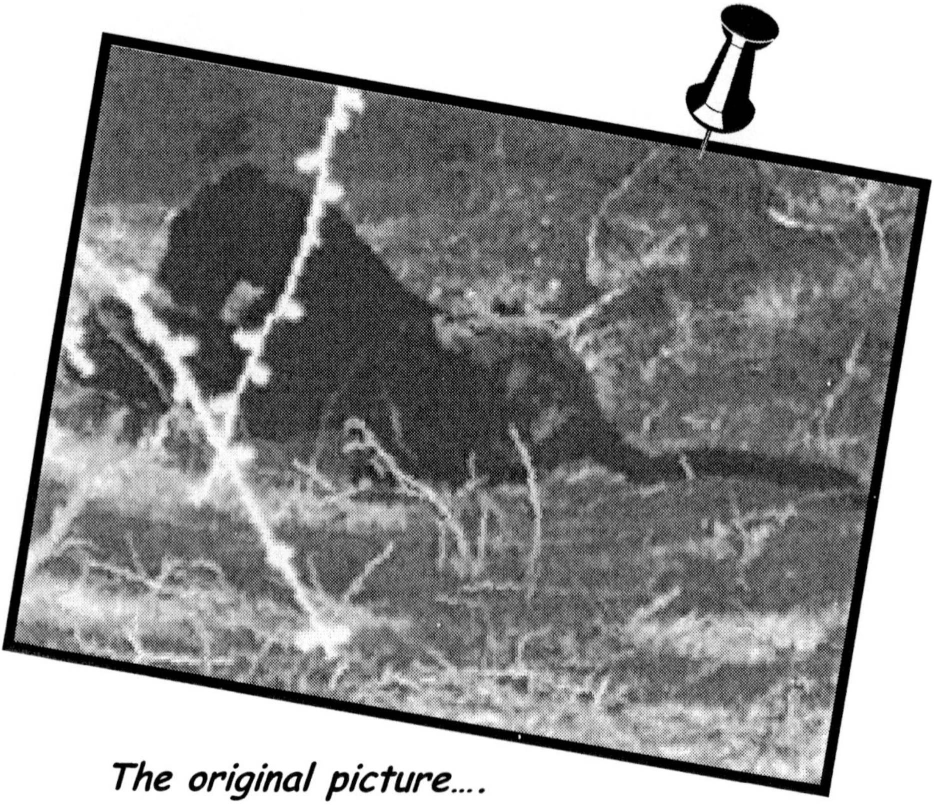

The original picture....

THE LAND OF WIZARDS, WITCHES AND DRAGONS TRIES TO ADD BIG CATS TO ITS LIST OF TOURIST ATTRACTIONS

In the world of Abnormal Big Cats there is one final location that requires investigation and that is the Principality of Wales. At this point things get a little dodgy. If you are able to read what I am about to write, then the editors and the legal people have OK'd what I am about to write; if you don't read it or it isn't here then it has been edited out in an effort to protect someone - probably me - from legal action.

Wales first appeared on my radar a few years ago with the case of a minor who had an encounter very similar to our friend in London, and for near enough the same reasons I dismissed it as a hoax, especially as the minor still had his face attached to his skull, which in turn was still attached to the rest of his body, but most surprising of all for a kid attacked by a puma/panther, he was still alive.

All I could think of was the Sherlock Holmes mystery, which had been on television that summer, the one, where the Mail Man did it using a fireside rake with four prongs on it. I'll leave it to you to read your Sherlock Holmes to find

out which story I mean.

This time I am looking at a picture of a Welsh panther. Yep a picture of a cat with multiple breaks in its tail, and the pitch black head and fore quarters; it *must* be a panther! How could it be anything else? Then there are the dubious quotes from the intrepid photographer, who firstly says he came upon the cat fifteen feet away, and then says he crawled up to the cat and from fifteen feet away he took two digital photographs.

I could not believe that a paper like the *Sun* could be taken in by such an image. Reports have it that the photographer took two pictures of the cat using his digital camera, which judging from the images, had an automatic flash built in to it. I can tell this because there are some badly over exposed bits of foliage in the foreground. So what else did I deduce from the images? And what practical experiments did I conduct to back up my suspicions?

Well:-

A) I fired up my digital camera (using brand new batteries) and fired off a flash and even with the new batteries it took several seconds to recharge the camera ready for the next exposure.

B) Now just think for a second. There you are - a large black cat happily munching away on the pigeon you have just plucked, and some idiot fires a flash off at you. You have two thoughts going through your head. Do I turn on the idiot with the camera? Or do I get the hell out of here? Either way I don't think I would be still sitting munching on the pigeon by the time the man's camera has recharged.

C) There were other puzzling aspects to the picture. There were shadows under the cat's head, and yet the cat's fore quarters were pitch black. I am sorry, but you can not have pitch black detail-less areas of an image, and have shadows under them at the same time! We live on earth - where there is a sun - and where there is a sun, there are shadows. Where the sun shines on a surface, it reveals details, but somehow these simple facts do not appear to apply in Wales. In Wales the sun shining on a surface produces shadows underneath the surface, but according to the photographic evidence supplied by this intrepid photographer the sun does not illuminate the surface it is shining on sufficiently to reveal detail. Quick send in the scientists to examine this phenomenon!

D) The photographer - who was quoted as saying he would not go back into the wood in case the panther was still there - did go back into the woods to have a nice picture taken of himself by another photographer. This means that the *Sun* not only printed the photograph taken by him, but in addition they printed a picture of him.

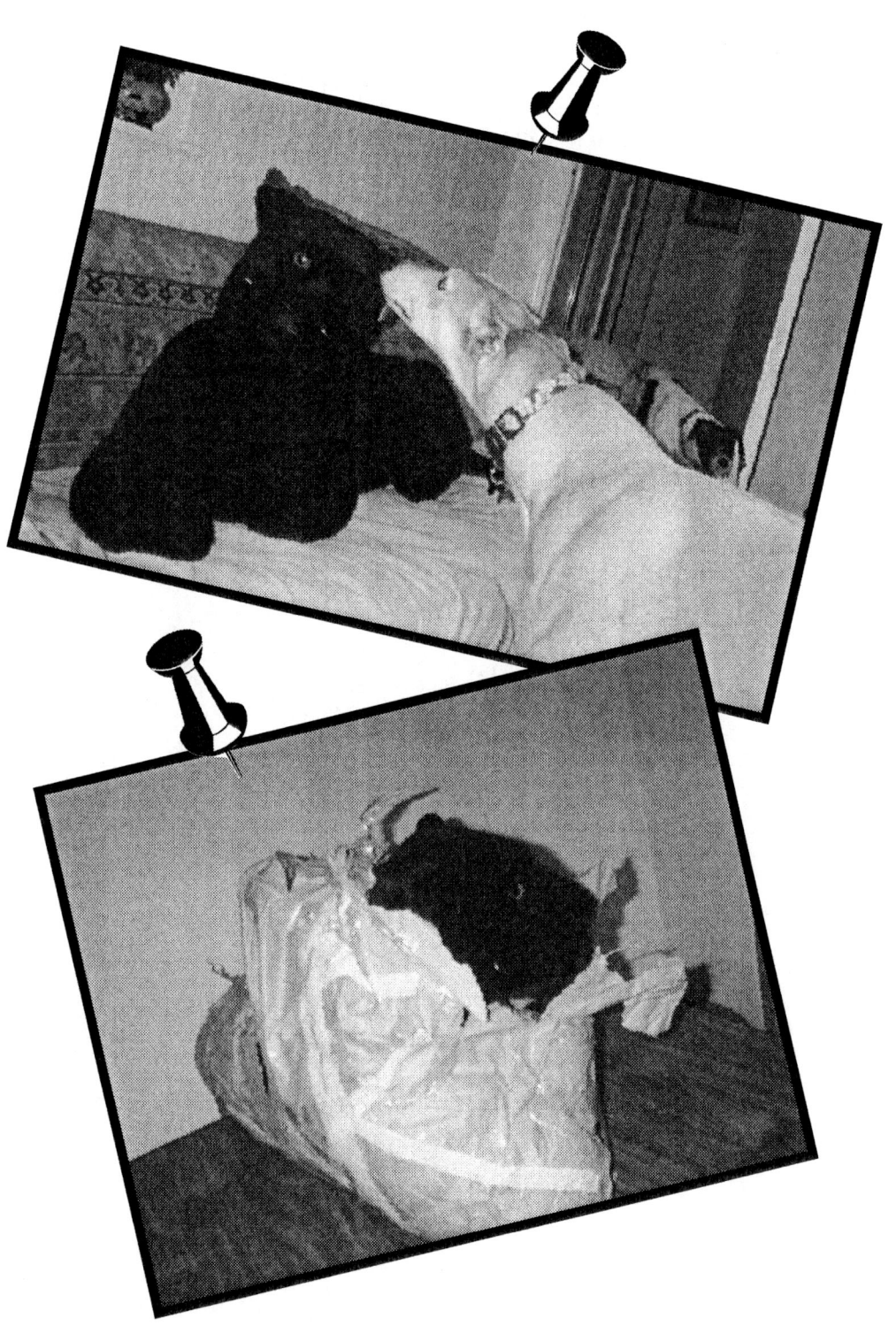

He's so brave, this photographer. If only the photographer knew what he had *really* photographed, I have to write that I am coming to the unprecedented conclusion that if this man is to be believed then he has had the unbelievable good fortune to photograph the ultimate in cryptozoology sightings: This photographer has captured on a silicon chip in his digital camera the first and very likely the only ever image of ...... an Anti-Vampire panther!

This unique image is of a panther, but a very special panther .... One which produces shadows but has no texture when light shines on it. Undoubtedly this is one of the rarest sights on earth and yet here our intrepid photographer has captured it on silicon for all to see. As you may have guessed by now I am running out of words to express my incredulity at such an occurrence, so I had better stop.

TWO HUMPS ARE BETTER THAN ONE!

It would appear that I was not the only one distressed by such a dodgy panther image; my mate Chris got the hump as well. In fact his hump was bigger than mine - you might go as far as to say he was a two-humped camel! Chris was/is convinced that the image is that of a large toy panther he saw in a market somewhere or other (but he can't remember where), but it might have been in a market in Exeter at Christmas.

To add to Chris's hump, his information concerning the *Sun's* image of a supposed Welsh panther on page 8 of the Saturday 16th April 2005 edition was not received by the features desk in a very courteous manor, in fact to quote Chris: "They were bloody rude!".

Now there is nothing guaranteed to upset Chris more than when he knows he holds the moral high ground, and you are rude to him. This camel was rapidly growing a third hump! So what was to be done? That was the question running through his head.

Chris's answer was to take out a complaint against the *Sun* newspaper for printing a false image. Naturally Chris used all the letters he has after his name, but featuring his FZS (Fellow of Zoological Society) and his membership of several zoological societies and publishing record. All this was done via the Press Complaints Commission.

Meanwhile, back in Cornwall, I was getting rather hacked off that people were getting good money for these images I'm thinking it was time to do one of my own, and as Steve Miller says:"Take the money and run". Unfortunately, Chris with his array of humps, got to me before I could act.

His idea was to use a toy panther, and catalogue our faking of the image, but as with all good ideas there was a snag ... you guessed it – we couldn't find a toy cat.

Instead we went to Porfell Animal Land, and spent the day watching Baz and Amy - the caracals - playing in their enclosure. It is surprising how calming it is watching the cats play, and now - apart from writing this - I am so serene, I don't give a monkey's about the *Sun's* photo.

Unfortunately, Chris has not found the inner calm that swept over me; he carried on looking for a toy panther, apparently his search for said toy took him to the northern reaches of the British Isles, where he reckons that someone in Scotland can get him one!

What Paul and Chris Did Next!

Sure enough, a week later the phone goes, and it is Chris telling me that he has got his toy cat.

So on a very sunny Wednesday 8th June 2005, the pair of us met up at Porfell. Chris had shown off his toy cat to every visitor, and the owners of Porfell by the time I arrived. His enthusiasm was such that the girl behind the counter didn't bother with the usual: "Hello and Welcome to Porfell", no, she just said "you must be the photographer, your friend dropped that off-" (pointing to the toy cat) "and he has run off to the woods, saying you can find him there!"

I went into the Zoo in search of John Palmer - the owner of Porfell - to let him know that the 'chaos brothers' were here. and drag him away from his work for a cup of coffee. Despite being a man of action, I thought it was better for me to drink coffee with John and wait for Chris to return. To be honest it was far too hot for me to go running into the woods after him.

Anyhow, I have put on a monumental amount of weight since I gave up smoking my pipe several months ago, and while the exercise would do me good, quite frankly I couldn't be arsed! I knew the smell of coffee was always more likely to attract Chris to my location, than me successfully locate him in the vast acreage of Porfell woods.

Sure enough, my coffee ploy worked. and it was much to Chris's surprise that I told him where I was going to photograph the toy; namely beside the pond/lake, taking the photographs through the trees so that I could use them to give the pictures that air of mystery, by using the tree's foliage to semi-obscure the toy. In

other words, there had been no sense in him rushing off scouting for locations.

As we drank our coffees, I joked about having to go back up the road to get a "road kill" badger to place between the toy's paws. There was a scraping of John's chair on the wooden floor, and he was gone.

Sixty seconds later John was back at the table with a carrier bag which he furtively passed around the table. The result was what can aptly be described as "James Bond " smirks all round and a frozen dead rabbit in a carrier bag.

Half an hour and one roll of film later, we were back consuming more coffee. John and I had taken digital cameras with us in my case so I could preview the images taken of the toy, and even on a screen one inch square, things were looking good. After a celebratory pasty, I was on my way home having entrusted Chris with the development of my film. To find out what happened next you will have to wait for the next thrilling instalment of the adventures of *The Beast and I*....................................

Is this not the best fake big cat picture you have ever seen?

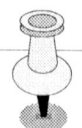

About the author............

Paul Crowther has taught photography since 1988. He is currently a photographic consultant for the Centre for Fortean Zoology, and is a multi-competition winner, having won prizes in zoological, scientific and environmental classes. He is a tutor and examiner for Amateur Photographer and was responsible for debunking the "Cornish Puma" picture from 1996. He subsequently found the animal, and discovered it to be an Abyssinian (domestic) cat.

Not appearing, but slightly to the right: Michaela Strachan

About the cartoonist...

MIECZYSŁAW KUCZYŃSKI
An appreciation by the writer

My Father in Law, or, Mr. K, as I am allowed to call him, has had an adventurous life to say the least. He was deported to Siberia as a youth thanks to the Russian occupation of the area of Poland he lived in. Upon his release from this Hell he charged backwards and forewords across the Sahara Desert chasing Rommel before entering Montē Casino as a Bombardier with the Polish Army. His exploits during this time in his life can be followed in his cartoon book which shows his alternative view of the second world war entitled "Dzieje 2 Korpusu ... Inaczej." You won't be able to understand a word of it but the cartoons are superb and very funny.

Having looked through Mr. K's numerous publications, it struck me that perhaps Mr. K was one of the most frequently photographed individual of the second world war, and if he was not the subject of the photograph he some how or other was in close proximity to the event being photographed for historical posterity.

This close proximity to historical events being captured on film led to his familiar caption under many of the illustrations in his numerous books ... "not visible in this photograph is M. Kuczyński." Mr. K will then patiently tell you what the event being photographed was and point out why he was not centre stage for the image, and if the photographer had moved slightly to the left or right then he instead of this idiot "X" would have been in the photograph.

THE CENTRE FOR FORTEAN ZOOLOGY

The Centre for Fortean Zoology is the world's only professional and scientific organisation dedicated to research into unknown animals. Although we work all over the world, we carry out regular work in the United Kingdom and abroad, investigating accounts of strange creatures.

THAILAND 2000
An expedition to investigate the legendary creature known as the Naga

SUMATRA 2003
'Project Kerinci'
In search of the bipedal ape Orang Pendek

MONGOLIA 2005
'Operation Death Worm'
An expedition to track the fabled 'Allghoi Khorkhoi' or Death Worm

Led by scientists, the CFZ is staffed by volunteers and is always looking for new members.

To apply for a <u>FREE</u> information pack about the organisation and details of how to join, plus information on current and future projects, expeditions and events.

Send a stamp addressed envelope to:

**THE CENTRE FOR FORTEAN ZOOLOGY
MYRTLE COTTAGE, WOOLSERY,
BIDEFORD, DEVON, EX39 5QR.**

or alternatively visit our website at: w w w . c f z . o r g . u k

Other books available from CFZ PRESS

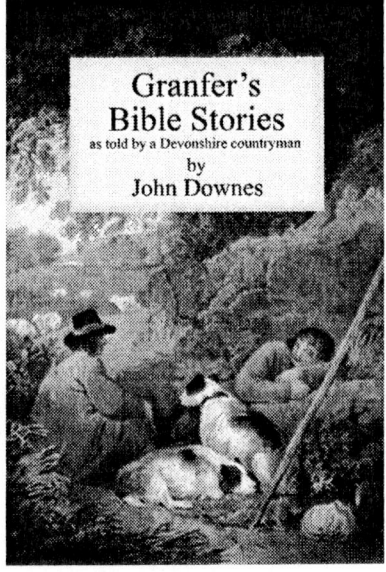

GRANFER'S BIBLE STORIES

Bible stories in the Devonshire vernacular, each story being told by an old Devon Grandfather - 'Granfer'. These stories are now collected together in a remarkable book presenting selected parts of the Bible as one more-or-less continuous tale in short 'bite sized' stories intended for dipping into or even for bed-time reading. `Granfer` treats the biblical characters as if they were simple country folk living in the next village. Many of the stories are treated with a degree of bucolic humour and kindly irreverence, which not only gives the reader an opportunity to re-evaluate familiar tales in a new light, but do so in both an entertaining and a spiritually uplifting manner.

ISBN 0-9512872-81

WHILE THE CAT'S AWAY

Over the past thirty years or so there have been numerous sightings of large exotic cats, including black leopards, pumas and lynx, in the South West of England. Former Rhodesian soldier Sam McCall moved to North Devon and became a farmer and pub owner when Rhodesia became Zimbabwe in 1980. Over the years despite many of his pub regulars having seen the "Beast of Exmoor" Sam wasn't at all sure that it existed. Then a series of happenings made him change his mind.

Chris Moiser—a zoologist—is well known for his research into the mystery cats of the Westcountry. This is his first novel.

ISBN: 0-9512872-14

Other books available from CFZ PRESS

MONSTER HUNTER
Jonathan Downes

Jonathan Downes' long-awaited autobiography, *Monster Hunter*...

Written with refreshing candour, it is the extraordinary story of an extraordinary life, in which the author crosses paths with wizards, rock stars, terrorists, and a bewildering array of mythical and not so mythical monsters, and still just about manages to emerge with his sanity intact.......

ISBN 0-9512872-7-3

DRAGONS
More than a myth?
Richard Freeman

First scientific look at dragons since 1884. It looks at dragon legends worldwide, and examines modern sightings of dragon-like creatures, as well as some of the more esoteric theories surrounding dragonkind. Dragons are discussed from a folkloric, historical and cryptozoological perspective, and Richard Freeman concludes that: "When your parents told you that dragons don't exist - they lied!"

ISBN 0-9512872-9-X

Other books available from CFZ PRESS

MONSTER OF THE MERE

It all starts on Valentine's Day 2002 when a Lancashire newspaper announces that "Something" has been attacking swans at a nature reserve in Lancashire. Eyewitnesses have reported that a giant unknown creature has been dragging fully grown swans beneath the water at Martin Mere.

An intrepid team from the Exeter based Centre for Fortean Zoology, led by the author, make two trips – each of a week – to the lake and its surrounding marshlands. During their investigations they uncover a thrilling and complex web of historical fact and fancy, quasi Fortean occurrences, strange animals and even human sacrifice.

ISBN 0-9512872-22

ONLY FOOLS AND GOATSUCKERS

In January and February 1998 Jonathan Downes and Graham Inglis of the Centre for Fortean Zoology spent three and a half weeks in Puerto Rico, Mexico and Florida, accompanied by a film crew from UK Channel 4 TV. Their aim was to make a documentary about the terrifying chupacabra - a vampiric creature that exists somewhere in the grey area between folklore and reality. This remarkable book tells the gripping, sometimes scary, and often hilariously funny story of how the boys from the CFZ did their best to subvert the medium of contemporary TV documentary making and actually do their job.

ISBN 0-9512872-30

Printed in the United Kingdom
by Lightning Source UK Ltd.
108253UKS00001B/381